Ethics and Internationa

CU00969275

B

Ethics and International Relations

Gordon Graham

BLACKWELL
Publishers

Copyright © Gordon Graham, 1997

The right of Gordon Graham to be identified as author of this work has been asserted in accordance with the Copyright, Designs and Patents Act 1988.

First published 1997

2 4 6 8 10 9 7 5 3 1

Blackwell Publishers Ltd
108 Cowley Road
Oxford OX4 1JF
UK

Blackwell Publishers Inc.
238 Main Street
Cambridge, Massachusetts 02142
USA

British Library Cataloguing in Publication Data

A CIP catalogue record for this book is available from the British Library.

Library of Congress Cataloging-in-Publication Data

Graham, Gordon.
  Ethics and international relations / Gordon Graham.
    p.   cm.
  Includes bibliographical references and index.
  ISBN 0-631-19682-X (hardcover: alk. paper). – ISBN 0-631-19683-8 (pbk.: alk. paper)
    1. International relations – Moral and ethical aspects.   I. Title.
JX1395.G66   1997
172'.4 – dc20   96-20831
                                                                                CIP

Typeset in 11½ on 13½ pt Bembo
by Best-set Typesetter Ltd, Hong Kong
Printed in Great Britain by Hartnolls Ltd, Bodmin, Cornwall

This book is printed on acid-free paper

Contents

Preface

This book is intended primarily for students in philosophy, politics and IR courses who want a general survey of the principal issues in ethics and international relations. It is written in a way that presupposes no previous knowledge of the subject, and it does not aim to be exhaustive. Both these requirements mean that necessarily the discussion is curtailed at points where there is more to be said. I have tried to indicate clearly where these points are, and striven to avoid simplifying complex questions. The intention is to be introductory without being elementary.

The amount of literature relevant to the topics of the book is enormous. Each chapter ends with suggestions for further reading, but these only scratch the surface. They have been chosen both for their accessibility to newcomers and, where it is possible to combine this consideration, from books and essays that have attracted critical discussion. Full details will be found in the bibliography at the end of the book.

I have benefited from having to lecture on these topics over a number of years to combined classes of philosophy and IR students, and am grateful for all the questions that have been raised in class. But special thanks are due to Lindsay Graham who read and commented on the whole text from the point of view of a student reader, and alerted me to several places in which the argument needed to be clarified.

Gordon Graham
University of Aberdeen

1

The International Order

From Vienna to Versailles:
the Rise of the Nation State

International society as we know it today is composed for the most part of self-governing nation states, and consequently world affairs consist in treaties, diplomatic relations, compacts and (relatively) occasional conflicts between them. This was not always so. Indeed, it was not so until quite recently. Throughout the nineteenth century and into the twentieth, the world was dominated by empires, not nation states. These empires incorporated very many different, and disparate, ethnic groups, governed by a ruling elite, often (though not always) drawn from just one nationality. For example, the affairs of hundreds of millions of people in Africa, Asia, North America and Australasia were controlled from London by the British, and the empire of the Ottoman Turks extended over most of North Africa, the Near East and parts of Europe for several centuries.

The rise of the nation state is, in fact, a modern phenomenon. We have only to recall the Greek and Roman, Mogul, Chinese, and Persian empires of the ancient world, the Holy Roman empire of the Middle Ages, and the Spanish, Portuguese, and Dutch as well as British and Ottoman empires of the early modern period, to realize that in this respect the nineteenth century was much more like other centuries than the twentieth. Such empires were not countries so much as power blocs, and while it is true that in this century international politics has also been in part a story of tension between power blocs, there is a difference. The period known as the Cold War was dominated by relations between Nato and the Warsaw Pact, but both the Warsaw Pact (in theory), and Nato (in reality) were combinations of independent states, not single empires.

The difference between the modern world and the world as it had been constituted for most of human history is strikingly marked if we compare the international orders which emerged from the Congress of Vienna (1815) and the Treaty of Versailles (1919). Both were major international political settlements. The Congress of Vienna marked the end of the Napoleonic wars. This period of strife in Europe was the outcome of the brilliant military exploits of Napoleon Bonaparte, who intended to estab-lish an empire, a far-flung grouping of nations, governed by the French with himself as Emperor. Napoleon's imperial ambitions, it should be underlined, were not at all extraordinary in his own day, as were, say, Hitler's in the twentieth century. Empire building was the norm. In resisting Napoleon, the British, Russians and Austrians were not resisting the *idea* of imperial rule, but the threat which this particular expansion of French power posed for their own territories and spheres of influence. This is reflected in the fact that the settlement of Europe which followed the Congress took account only of the balance of power between the then imperial rulers; the nations (i.e. ethnic groups) they ruled were not themselves of any great consequence. This struggle between empires continued to dominate nineteenth-century international politics. For the remainder of the century Britain sought to defend its empire in India against the threats it saw coming from the expansion of the Russian empire into Central Asia. What was known as 'The Great Game' of espio-nage and counter-espionage was played out between these two powers for several decades. It continued to be played in the early years of this century between Britain and Germany, many of the adventure stories of John Buchan being based on the spying and intrigue which the covert struggle between the British and the Germans generated.

This imperial conception of international order, shared by all the parties to the Congress of Vienna, stands in very sharp contrast to the principles invoked in the Treaty of Versailles which concluded World War I. At the Paris Peace Conference, where the Treaty was agreed, President Woodrow Wilson of the United States insisted that the rights of nations to self-determination should play a significant part. State boundary lines were to be drawn, not in accordance with the requirements of the balance of power between imperial blocs (or not solely), but in accordance with national identity. This was a principle of which other negotiators at the Conference were sceptical, notably the French Prime Minister, Clemenceau, and, as a result, the political map which emerged was only partially constructed in this way. But the fact that the basic unit for the international order should be taken to be the nation, an idea which would have been ridiculous one hundred years previously, shows what a significant change had occurred in the course of the nineteenth century in the nature of international relations.

This dramatic change was in large part the outcome of the spread of political nationalism. Nationalism takes many forms, cultural as well as political, but a central, almost defining, belief of political nationalism is the doctrine that each nation should constitute a state in itself. In the elaboration of this doctrine, the criterion of nationhood – what makes a nation – is obviously crucial. In the early period of nationalism, its theorists argued that the definitive characteristic was language, and though after a time a broader and looser definition came to be used, national identity structured around a common language continued to play a very large part. The formation of Germany out of many minor principalities made a common language its principle of unification; language featured prominently in the struggle for Italian independence from the Austro-Hungarian empire, Greece from the Turkish empire, Iceland from Denmark, and its revival was one (unrealized) aim of Irish independence from Britain. But even in the absence of a common language political nationalism came to dominate thinking about the international order, so much so that most people now take it for granted that international relations are relations between nation states.

Arguably the very possibility of a subject called 'ethics in international affairs' is one important outcome of this change of thinking. When the world was governed along imperial lines, moral considerations did enter into political debate, but principally with respect to the relations between heads of state on the one hand, and ruler and ruled on the other, not between nations and peoples. The ethics of making and keeping agreements between kings and emperors was always of importance, and, in the past, philosophers and theologians often wondered about what moral limits restrained a Christian prince in the treatment of enemies and governance of the peoples subjected to his rule. This question continued to be of consequence even when the term 'Christian prince' was no longer strictly applicable. Was Britain, for instance, as a Christian country, entitled, or perhaps even obliged to convert to Christianity the Hindu and Moslem subject peoples of the Indian sub–continent? In arriving at a policy on this issue – Christian missionaries were given the protection but not the support of the state – the British government of the nineteenth century tended to mix principles with pragmatism, but the principles invoked had to do with the duty of the ruler and the welfare of the subject. If the imperial powers acted (more or less) decently and to the benefit, or at least not the gross disbenefit, of their subject peoples, this was sufficient.

Against this background, nationalist aspirations introduced a quite novel ethical notion – the rights of peoples. Nationalists pre-eminently claimed the right of self-determination of peoples, by which was meant ethnic groups. This lent a special sort of justice to their cause, for even when subject peoples were not being ill-treated, though unquestionably they often were, the fact that they were not self-governing was in itself a moral grievance. The nation state thus became an expression of an ethical ideal – the right of each nation to rule over itself – and the history of the twentieth century can in large measure be seen to be an outcome of the prominence, prestige and popularity of this idea. The Allied victory over Hitler in World War II, for instance, can be regarded as a defeat of the last openly expressed ambition to form a *Reich* or empire. By the middle part of the century, the power of nationalism was illustrated by the rapid demise of the Dutch, French, Portuguese and most notably British empires, as more and more of their subject peoples claimed the right to self-government.

Even with the demise of recognized empires, the persuasiveness of the ideal of *national* independence has continued, as is further illustrated by claims made by emerging nation states and their supporters about *covert* American imperialism. In the last third of this century, the aspiration to self-government has lain at the heart of most (though not all) liberation groups and terrorist campaigns, Basque separatists and the IRA being amongst the most notable examples, and generated dramatic civil strife in the former composite states of Yugoslavia and the Soviet Union.

The right of national self-determination, if there is such a right, is not a *legal* right, a right bestowed by international law. It should be thought of first and foremost, rather, as a *moral* right, because in so far as international law does not enshrine it, its proponents would hold that it ought to do so. Indeed, the belief in a right *more fundamental* than international law, which international law *ought* to respect, explains the terms of many modern international agreements, including the United Nations Charter. In this respect the right of self-determination is similar to the human rights of individuals, upon which there have been many international declarations.

The importance of the idea that nations have moral rights, of which the most important is the right to self-government, can hardly be exaggerated. It colours almost all thinking about ethics in international affairs. This is because it has been extended beyond the bare right of statehood, to include rights which protect and promote it, rights relating to humanitarian intervention, distributive justice and the environment. Taken together these concerns form much of the subject matter of ethics in international affairs and hence many of the topics examined in this book. To consider these properly, however, it is necessary to begin by examining the general idea that nation states are moral units with significant rights. One way of doing this is to look at the merits of alternative ways of thinking, ways that might be described as internationalist.

The Challenge of Internationalism

One of these is the imperialism out of which nationalism arose. In the late twentieth century it is extremely unfashionable to advance the cause of imperialism. What was commonplace, even in the late nineteenth century – that imperialism is a natural and respectable form of government – is now by and large unsupportable. Yet the claims of imperial government are not so easily dismissed as most people are inclined to think. Imperialism is decried, very often, not so much because of its intrinsic nature, but because of the racist ideas and commercial greed associated with it, a combination whose deep unpleasantness is powerfully conveyed by Joseph Conrad in the novel *Heart of Darkness*. There is no doubt that Western imperialists of the eighteenth and nineteenth centuries thought that some nationalities, notably Africans and those on the Indian sub-continent, were unfit to govern themselves. It is worth noting, however, that racism itself is an idea that appears relatively late in the history of imperialism. In fact we can leave these racist beliefs aside, because they are not central to the idea of imperial government itself, which can more simply be considered as a rejection of the alternative of national self-government itself, a rejection, that is to say, of the idea that nationality is the best basis for good government.

Construed in this way, there are at least two things to be said in imperialism's favour. The Congress of Vienna, which settled Europe on imperial lines, was followed by a long period of relative peace. Although international tensions between the Great Powers of the nineteenth century continued, and developed into outright strife in the Crimean War, for the most part the settlement arrived at in Vienna secured peace and stability. In sharp contrast, the political settlement which emerged from the Paris Peace Conference rapidly proved to be unstable. In only twenty years world war broke out again. This cannot be blamed entirely on nationalism. The causes are complex, and include Hitler's imperialistic ambitions, though these were themselves fed by German nationalism, and exacerbated by absurd racist theories. Still, the attempt to redraw the political boundaries of Europe in accordance with the ideal of the self-determining nation state gave rise to competing claims to statehood which quickly generated widespread strife and then armed conflict. The same phenomenon followed the demise of the Ottoman empire – witness the conflicts of the Middle East, and the end of the British empire, especially on the Indian sub-continent where rivalry between India, Pakistan and Bangladesh has continued. In short, a true imperialist, if there were any left, could argue with some justice that the idea of the right of national self-determination has not ushered in a lasting international order, but destabilized the one that preceded it.

This observation is important because any justificatory theory of international relations must secure political success as well as political rights. Any international order requires stability and peace; war is the ultimate mark of failure in international affairs, and arguably, the right of nations to self-government has been a cause of war more often than the conflict of empires. Empires can produce very long-lasting periods of relative peace and order. A striking instance is the Roman empire, from whose collapse it took Europe a long time to recover. It is true that not infrequently this peace and order was purchased by means of great brutality, but many post-imperial governments of the twentieth century can scarcely escape the charge of brutality either. It is also true that political freedom as we understand it today was something which the peoples of the Roman, Russian or Chinese empires did not enjoy, but then, neither is it enjoyed by people caught up in international conflict or civil strife. Why, an imperialist might ask, should we insist on *self* government in preference to *good* government?

Second, there is a case to be made that imperialism is more realistic, because imperialistic ambitions are inevitable. History since time immemorial has been a story of the rise and fall of empires. Even in the course of this century, the language of national self-determination has been used to cloak empire building. With this in mind, it can seem foolishly idealistic for those who believe in the right of national self-determination to think that such a radical alteration in the ways of the world, and of those who aspire to rule it, is possible. From this point of view, the doctrine of national self-determination is simply unrealistic as a lasting basis for international affairs, even if it is founded on ideas of justice and rights.

The clash between realism and moralism in international relations is one of the main topics of the next chapter. For the moment, however, let us concentrate on the two points which seem to favour imperialism: (1) experience shows that imperial government produces a more stable international order; and (2) we have no reason to favour nationalistic integrity over peace and stability.

It is unlikely that these two points briefly stated will make the claims of imperialism convincing. Imperialism is too far out of favour, and too closely associated with racism and brutality, for the claim that imperial government is better government to carry much weight. The most familiar image of imperialistic ambition is of someone like Genghis Khan (*c.*1162–1227), the Mongol conqueror who established his rule over vast territories by a military campaign of almost unsurpassed ferocity, and this is hardly a model which is likely to commend itself. Unfashionable ideas, of course, are not false because unfashionable. Even so, it is unlikely that imperialism can be raised to respectability, and in any case it is not necessary. The fundamental challenge of interest here which imperialism presents to contemporary ways of thinking about international affairs, is not unique to imperialism. Indeed, it is not the claims of *imperialism* as such which need to be addressed, but the claims of *internationalism*. The title 'Khan' means 'Universal Ruler' and this suggests a link between imperialism and alternative forms of internationalism, which otherwise seem quite unconnected with it.

One of these is communism, a quite different form of internationalism. Much of the history of the twentieth century is marked by the spread of communism. This is now in decline, but it is worth observing that communism set out to be an international doctrine. That is to say, communist theory, as elaborated by Marx and more especially Lenin, held that political and economic interests transcend national boundaries. It is no accident that the most famous slogan of the Communist Manifesto is for the workers *of the world* to unite, or that the Congresses at which communists gathered were known as 'Internationals'. Marx believed that nationalistic divisions were part of an ideological superstructure which served to disguise the real nature of economic relations and hence political affairs and that for workers to have nationalistic loyalties was contrary to their true interests. In his view, the promotion of widespread belief in the right of national self-determination was just one more instrument in the armoury of international capitalism, which along with others allowed it to continue to divide and rule.

So large a part did internationalism play in the foundations of communism, that at first it was believed that communism could not succeed in just one country. When Stalin, having failed to stimulate revolution on a European wide scale, finally accepted the (interim) aim of 'socialism in one country', this was regarded by many communists as a sign of failure and by nearly all as an unfortunate second best. Arguably, of course, Stalin's 'socialism in one country' was itself something of a smokescreen for the continuance of Russian imperialism, since the Union of Soviet Socialist Republics, and then the Eastern bloc, was in reality more a forced political amalgamation of disparate nations dominated by Russians than a willing combination of peoples inspired by the socialist ideal. But whatever the truth about this, its internationalist, if not its imperial, character was consistent with communist theory, because of the fundamental belief that national divisions are not of real significance.

No doubt the decline of communism and the history of Stalin's Russia do little to enhance the claims of internationalism or to tarnish the appeal of the nation state. But to regard the matter as settled is to ignore the fact that one reason for thinking badly of communism is its failure to live up to the internationalist ideal of its orginators. Despite first appearances then, there is significant common ground between imperialism and communism. In contrast to the doctrine of the nation state, both are internationalist doctrines, and the merits of this shared component can, in fact, be considered in isolation from either imperialist aggression or communist totalitarianism. This is because internationalism in a third form continues to play an important role in the world politics of this century, this third form being what is sometimes called 'cosmopolitanism'.

The word 'cosmopolitan' comes from the Greek words for 'world' and 'city', and so it is no surprise that the most ambitious form of cosmopolitanism is 'world government'. This ambition is sometimes dismissed as a piece of fantasy, because it certainly seems that the formation of a world government, if it ever happens, is very far away indeed. However, there are two good reasons for not dismissing cosmopolitanism out of hand. The first is that in the area of ethics and international relations we are not concerned primarily with the practical reality of political programmes, but with the moral desirability of political ideals. In the end, of course, the two must come together, and we will be concerned with a more detailed treatment of this subject in the next chapter. Our first task, though, is to test the *ideal* of national statehood by considering the merits of its most plausible rival. Second, it may be true that fully fledged world government is still a remote possibility, but cosmopolitanism can and does find expression in more modest institutions, early steps along the way so to speak. Some of these have played a very important part in the international politics of the twentieth century. We can only assess the merits of these first moves if we make some estimation of the value of the goal they imply, and this is what makes the idea of world government one worth exploring.

Chief among the tentative movements towards world government which the twentieth century has witnessed was the formation, after World War I, of the League of Nations, and, after World War II, its successor the United Nations. Many people have serious doubts about the extent to which the United Nations has realized the aspirations of its founders. Has it been anything more than a rather expensive, high profile, talking shop? Important though this question is, it is not the issue to be considered here. What the United Nations represents, on any understanding, is the aspiration of creating an international forum which will transcend national boundaries and so serve as a means of regulating international affairs. The possible roles for such a body are several – the promotion of co-operative action on matters of mutual interest and the existence of a forum for the discussion and resolution of conflicting interests are two obvious possibilities. Both have to a degree been realized. But much more interesting from a theoretical point of view is the idea that the UN might serve as an 'international policeman'. What makes this interesting is that it implies, ultimately, the transfer of sovereignty from national to international level. That is to say, if the United Nations were to act in an *enforcing* and not merely a deliberative role, something after the fashion that it seemed to do during the Gulf War of 1990–1, this would imply that nation states are not the repositories of ultimate power and authority. In short, nation states would cease to be sovereign in certain important respects.

Would this matter? Here we encounter, at last, the real challenge that internationalism, now in the form of cosmopolitanism, presents to a nation-based world order. From the cosmopolitan point of view, there is no reason to regard national groupings as the rightful, or most suitable unit for sovereignty. If there is a right of national self-determination, it is not an absolute right, and must take second place to international sovereignty.

Sovereignty

Sovereignty is a central political concept. A political body is sovereign in so far as it alone has the authority to be ultimate decision maker, to have, we might say, the last word. In so far as a political body, a town council say, is subject to the authority of some other body, Parliament or Congress for example, it is not sovereign. It does *not* have the last word. To grasp the concept of sovereignty properly, it is essential that we distinguish power from authority. There is an age-old doctrine that 'might makes right', which compounds the two, since it holds that to have the *power* to make effective decisions implies the *authority* to do so. It does not take very much critical reflection, however, to see that

there is an inherent implausibility in this. It seems very clear that
the *rightful* exercise of decisions can be brushed aside by the use
of military power, without thereby losing any of its rightfulness.
A constitutionally elected government, for instance, could be
(and history is full of examples) subjected to a *coup d'état* by force
of arms, even when there cannot be any serious doubt that the
seizure is unlawful. In such circumstances, the success of the *coup*
leaves its perpetrators with power, but not with authority. They
may of course successfully exercise political control of the country in question. Then, in the language of the law, they govern *de
facto*, as a matter of fact, but not *de jure*, not lawfully, or by right.

Cases like this lend support to the intuitive conviction that
power and authority are conceptually distinct. Intuitive conviction is not argument, however, but the French political philosopher Jean-Jacques Rousseau (1712–78), in the *Social Contract*,
provides an argument to the same conclusion. In the chapter
entitled 'The Right of the Strongest' he writes:

> Let us suppose for a moment that this alleged right is valid. I say
> that the result would be completely senseless. For as soon as right
> is founded on force, the effect will alter with its cause; any force
> that is stronger than the first must have right on its side in its turn.
> As soon as anyone is able to disobey with impunity he may do so
> legitimately, and since the strongest is always right the only
> question is how to ensure that one is the strongest. But what kind
> of right is it that is extinguished when that strength is lost? If we
> must obey because of force we have no need to obey out of duty,
> and if we are no longer forced to obey we no longer have any
> obligation to do so. It can be seen therefore that the word 'right'
> adds nothing to force; it has no meaning at all here. (*Social
> Contract*, Ch. iii)

Rousseau offers us a simple but convincing argument that rights
and might are necessarily distinct. It follows that to be concerned
with establishing the proper basis of right and wrong, is to be
concerned with the source of political authority, not the source
of political power. The workings of political power can be said to
be the subject matter of political history and political science.
The central question of political philosophy is the foundation of

political right, which can be possessed by the weak as well as the powerful. In this respect, politics is no different to more homely cases. A school bully can use brute force to take the property of other pupils; it does not mean that she has any right to it.

Sovereignty is the stopping place of authority. This is why it is such an important political concept. A sovereign is one who has the last rightful say on all matters falling within its competence. In politics this means the lawful use of coercion. The British Parliament or the American Congress is sovereign, for instance, just in so far as it may rightfully use coercive power to enforce its decisions. Those who oppose such decisions are not merely subject to the power of the state, which usually they are, but to the *rightful* power of the state.

Given this distinction between power and authority, a question naturally arises as to where ultimate authority or sovereignty should rest. The dispute between nationalism and internationalism may be cast in this way, therefore. Nationalism holds that each nation should be sovereign over its affairs; internationalism holds that national concerns are rightly subject to international interests. These interests include, of course, international peace, but also international justice and the concerns of the global environment.

Federalism and the International 'State of Nature'

The analysis so far has shown this. The common and familiar assumption that international relations are relations between sovereign nation states is a peculiarity of the twentieth century. It is an assumption which conflicts both with imperialism, the prevailing idea of most periods of the past, and with the more modern doctrine of cosmopolitanism – the idea of the world as a unity, a sort of 'global village' which cannot be cut up into arbitrary national units. Both imperialism and cosmopolitanism are internationalist conceptions. That is to say, they share the view that the interests of international order may override the interests of any one nation state, and that when the two conflict, the latter may rightfully be made to give way to the former. Nationalism, by contrast, holds that it is the nation state which is ultimately sovereign.

To adjudicate in this dispute properly, we need to enquire into the source of the authority which internationalism claims. Consider the contrast with imperialism once more. We saw earlier that imperialism, despite its current unfashionableness, can take at least some justificatory credit from the fact that there is plausible evidence, by and large, of imperial government's being more stable and peaceful than its nationalist alternative. The political situation resulting from the rivalry of nations clamouring for statehood has very often been one of violence and instability. Nor is this a feature merely of the far-flung empires of the past. The collapse of the Soviet empire had this effect, as did the demise of Tito's Yugoslavia.

But, if this is indeed the best case for imperialism, it means in effect that the source of imperial authority is a modified version of the 'might is right' doctrine. The imperialist's strongest argument is this: good government is effective government to the extent that it secures peace and stability, and imperial government is effective; *ergo*, imperial government is good government. So far as it goes, this is a valid argument, but we should note that if and when imperial government has been effective, this has been the outcome of power. The great empires of the past were ruled, in the end, by force of arms. Their origins lay in conquest and their continuance in suppression of revolt. It is for this reason people often think that imperialism was unqualifiedly bad, though imperial force of arms not infrequently resulted in good things. For instance, British rule in East Africa, whatever its faults, was in fact better for the inhabitants of that area than was the rule of indigenous tyrants, such as Idi Amin, which followed it. The best objection to imperialism, then, is not that it was always harsh, but that even when it was good, it still rested on sheer power. Imperial rulers have no claim or entitlement to the lands they occupy other than the fact that they have forcibly occupied them. When imperial rule is effective, this does indeed generate a claim to the loyalty of its subjects. Empires ruled well,

often, because they were able to subdue local inhabitants, including, importantly, rival native factions. By this suppression, and
because of its beneficial consequences, imperial rulers usually had
the *acquiescence* of those they ruled. But what they did not have,
and would not have thought of seeking, was their *consent*. It
is this that makes imperialism a version of the 'might is right'
doctrine. When force of arms failed, which in almost every case
it eventually did, there was no other claim to authority.

What then of the other version of internationalism we have
been considering, namely, cosmopolitanism. If we take the prototype of cosmopolitan government to be the United Nations, a
body to which individual states are admitted on request and with
the agreement of other nations, we can say that cosmopolitanism,
in contrast to imperialism, gives pride of place to consent and
agreement. Consequently, when an international body of this sort
acts against an individual state, as the UN did against Iraq in the
Gulf War, its authority rests not simply on might, but on the
majority agreement of consenting members of what is nowadays
referred to as the international community.

The UN is not an example but at best a prototype of the
much more ambitious idea of world government. The legitimacy
which agreement lends to the actions of countries acting in
concert falls far short of a system under which the states of the
world would be bound together in such a way as would make
them subject to the authority, as well as the power, of a supreme
international sovereign body. The existence of such a body is a
long way off, but the basic structure it implies is a very familiar
one – federalism. In this respect the United States provides an
illuminating example, because, although we now tend to think of
it as a single national state, the US was formed from an original
compact or union between thirteen independent states, all of
which had achieved independence from British colonial rule. As
was to be expected, what emerged from this colonial experience
was an inter-state organization sharply in contrast to the imperial
order that it had sought to escape. The founding states agreed to
form a federation for certain purposes. These became matters for
the federal government. For other purposes they agreed to remain independent states, and these became matters of 'states'

rights'. As new territories gained state recognition, they were in turn admitted to the federation, which implied that henceforth they were both entitled to representation in federal government, and at the same time subject to its authority over federal matters.

The model of federalism the US provides is, we may suppose, a plausible model for any likely form of world government. Interestingly, it is also a political union very much in keeping with a longstanding tradition in political philosophy, one which was as a matter of fact highly influential in the drafting of the American Constitution. This tradition holds that the authority of rulers derives from the consent of the ruled. It is a conception to be found first made most articulate in the writings of the English philosopher John Locke (1632–1704). Locke is an important figure in political philosophy for having written *Two Treatises of Government*. The first Treatise aimed to refute the idea that kings rule by divine right, a view advocated by the Stuart monarchs of the recently united kingdoms of England and Scotland, and the second aimed to show that the authority of what Locke calls 'the magistrate', derives from the consent of those subject to magisterial authority. To demonstrate this conclusion, in the *Second Treatise* Locke engages in a sort of thought experiment. In order to discover the foundation of political authority, he imagines society without government (which he also seems to have thought did really exist at one time). This he calls 'the state of nature', and in the state of nature, Locke contends, because there is no government, there are no civil laws. There are, however, *natural* laws which, among other things, give individuals rights to property, self-defence and the punishment of wrongdoers. Now, since individuals may be too weak or too partial to enforce their natural rights properly, they have good reason to agree to hand over some of their rights to a central authority which will exercise them, and hence protect them, on their behalf. In so doing, according to Locke, they bring political society into being and put an end to the state of nature.

The central authority thus created is the magistrate or government, and its authority derives from citizens in just this sense; by their consent and agreement the government exercises *their* rights. In contrast to the doctrine of the Divine Right of Kings, on the individualist theory Locke defends, kings and governors have no special right of their own by which they are entitled to rule: both their right to govern, and the moral limits on the way they may do so, derive from the natural rights of their subjects.

The 'Domestic Analogy' in International Relations

Locke's political philosophy has been the subject of a very great deal of discussion. Many of its central elements were revived in contemporary philosophy, to considerable effect, by the American philosopher Robert Nozick in *Anarchy, State and Utopia* (1973). The question of its adequacy and plausibility is not the main issue here, however. What we need to ask in the present context is whether the basic picture Locke paints (which is a picture of first natural and then political relations between individual human beings) can be applied to relations between states.

On the face of it there is a good deal to be said for thinking that it can. Individuals in Locke's state of nature are sovereign. That is to say, they have the absolute right to decide matters for themselves, subject to the natural or moral rights of others, and they can only justifiably be constrained in this if by free consent they combine together under one authority or government which then exercises some of those rights on their behalf. In short, in electing a 'magistrate' to exercise their rights in the interests of justice and public order, they form a sort of association or federation.

Is the international position any different? The international order, in the absence of world government, is a sort of state of nature in which individual nation states are sovereign, that is, free to decide matters for themselves. But since any state may find itself too weak or inclined to self-interest, this can result in international moral disorder – aggression, war, plundering, espionage and so on. To avoid these evils, individual nation states, just like the individuals in Locke's state of nature, have reason to combine in a federation which results in institutions of international government more powerful and more authoritative than those of the nation state. The end result, in world society just as in any national society, is a rule of law which constrains individual behaviour in accordance with moral rights and international order, while at the same time leaving the individual nation state with some rights of its own.

This parallel between the national and the international is generally known as 'the domestic analogy'; that is to say, it draws an analogy between, on the one hand, the position with respect to government and rights in the domestic or one-country case, and the position in multi-state cases on the other. The point of doing so is to throw light on the ethics of international affairs. Moral right and wrong is generally clearer in the domestic case than in the international case. If we are reasonably clear about what fellow citizens may and may not do to each other, and what governments may and may not require of their citizens, and if the domestic analogy is a good one, we can extrapolate to an international context. We will then be able to tell what individual states may legitimately do with and to each other, what authority it makes sense to attribute to institutions of world or global government, and where the limits of that authority lie.

The 'domestic analogy', therefore, is a promising way forward, and one which many of those writing about ethics and international affairs have sought to exploit. There are, however, two very serious lines of objection that are commonly brought against it. The first is this. The Lockean idea of a state of nature, upon which ultimately the analogy rests, assumes that in a pre-political state, where there are no *civil* laws to regulate behaviour, there are, nonetheless, *moral* laws. That is to say, the world of Locke's state of nature is a moral world, to which the concepts of right and wrong (ultimately founded upon God, in Locke's view) apply, and where the task of political government, consequently, is to reflect these moral laws in its civil enactments.

Now this is a feature of the state of nature that has been disputed. An alternative conception is to be found in the writings of an earlier English political philosopher, Thomas Hobbes (1588–1679), whose idea of the state of nature is one in which there is *no* pre-political idea of right and wrong. Faced with the dispute between the Lockean and the Hobbesian conceptions of the state of nature, people's intuitions vary. On balance, however, most people will tend to agree with Locke. In effect, to do so is to agree that it is possible to do someone a wrong even where no criminal law has been promulgated against it. To see this, think of the state of nature as the condition of a few people shipwrecked on a deserted island. In such circumstances there is no government, no civil law. It nonetheless seems plausible to hold that one person can act wrongly with respect to the other, by aggressively stealing the food they have gathered, or breaking a promise to share firewood, say. If this does seem plausible, it follows that the state of nature between individuals, exemplified by this imaginary case, is *not* a moral vacuum, but one to which the ideas of moral right and wrong apply.

What has proved much less plausible to many theorists of international affairs, however, is the suggestion that the state of nature between *nations* is equally morally ordered. According to a school of thought generally known as 'realism', the international order is a Hobbesian, not a Lockean state of nature, one in which concepts of moral right and wrong do not apply, and where the sole consideration upon which international relations, including international co-operation, are to be conducted is one of national self-interest. Realism denies the relevance of the domestic analogy by claiming that whereas the relation between individuals in a state of nature *is* a moral one, the relation between states is *not*. In short, realism rejects moralism with respect to international affairs, and hence denies that there can be ethics in international affairs at all.

The second type of doubt about the domestic analogy is less sweeping than realism but not much less important. It questions, not so much whether there is an ethics of international affairs, but whether the moral framework appropriate to relations between individual human beings is relevant to relations between states. This doubt arises because, while there is some substance to an analogy between the two, there is even greater substance to a disanalogy. Two disanalogous features are striking. First, states are composed of many individuals, each with some moral standing of their own, but individual human beings have no parallel morally relevant 'sub–units'. Second, individuals have beliefs and can suffer pain and death. These are facts about them highly relevant to the moral laws which govern relations between human beings. They have no parallel, or no obvious parallel, however, in the case of states. Nation states do not have beliefs and they cannot be tortured or killed. Sceptics of the domestic analogy, whose reasoning follows this second line of thought, need not deny that ethical issues can arise in international affairs, but they do deny that these can be solved or settled upon the moral principles that govern relations between human beings.

Both these objections to the domestic analogy are of great consequence for the ethics of international affairs. If the first objection is correct, there can be no such thing; if the second is correct, we need to start thinking upon rather different lines. Either way, the relation between morality and the international order is special, and for this reason, the next chapter is devoted to exploring these objections and the issues they raise more closely.

Summary

Although we are inclined to think of international relations as relations between nation states, this way of thinking is very much a product of the twentieth century. It is to be contrasted both with the imperialism of the past, when international relations were relations between imperial powers, and with a cosmopolitan vision of the future when nation states will be bound together in a world federation to which they will be subject. Both imperialism and cosmopolitanism are internationalist doctrines which believe that sovereignty is not the exclusive prerogative of individual national groups, and that national boundaries are not the ultimate moral boundaries. Both doctrines permit the relegation of the nation state in the interests of a morally better international order.

The claims of imperialism are not without some credibility, but it is a very unfashionable doctrine. This is not necessarily a mark of falsehood, but it does mean that in the modern world it is cosmopolitanism that must be regarded as the principal rival to the sovereignty of the nation state. Cosmopolitanism's most plausible expression is in the idea of a world federation of states, formed by consenting nations for the purposes of co-operation, peace and a morally better ordered world. Exponents of this idea can draw upon the longstanding Lockean tradition in political philosophy which employs the concept of a state of nature out of which political society arises. In so doing they make use of a domestic analogy between political and moral relations between citizens and relations between states.

Doubts may be raised about this analogy, however. First, so-called 'realists' question whether the 'state of nature' between nations is not more Hobbesian than Lockean. Second, others question, in the light of important disanalogies, whether the moral principles that apply to relations between peoples are properly applicable to international relations at all. These doubts provide the topics of the next chapter.

Suggestions for further reading

(Full biographical details are to be found in the bibliography on p. 176.)

Charles R. Beitz, *Political Theory and International Relations*. An influential study of international relations from the point of view of contemporary political theory.

Hedley Bull, *The Anarchical Society*. A well known and well regarded text by a leading figure in the study of international relations.

L. C. B. Seaman, *From Vienna to Versailles*. A short book which gives a good overview of the dramatic changes in international affairs which took place over the course of the nineteenth century.

Peter Hopkirk, *The Great Game*. A highly readable account of the role of spying in the nineteenth-century struggle for empire in Central Asia between Britain and Russia.

Elie Kedourie, *Nationalism*. Kedourie is a convinced critic of nationalism, but his book provides a valuable combination of philosophical and historical reflection on the idea of the nation state.

John Locke, *Second Treatise of Government*. This is the *locus classicus* of political liberalism. Chapters I and II are those most relevant here.

2

International Morality

The Hobbesian State of Nature

The last chapter introduced the concept of a 'state of nature', the idea of a society before, or without, political government. What would such a society be like? There is a very famous phrase Hobbes uses to describe the state of nature. It is, he says, one in which life is 'solitary, poor, nasty, brutish and short'. His reason for thinking so is that in the state of nature, where there is neither rule of law nor anyone with the power to enforce it, anything goes. The natural right to possess property or pursue one's own purposes by any means available is, on Hobbes's account, not a right bestowed by a God-given natural law, but rather a 'natural liberty'. Given that there is no lawmaking authority, there can be no legal obstacles to doing whatever it is we want to do, and it is for this reason that Hobbes thinks that natural 'right' in such circumstances cannot mean more than simply an unfettered natural 'liberty'. Hobbes's state of nature, in contrast to Locke's, is not a state in which a different type of law operates, but one in which there is no law at all. Yet, such perfect liberty is not a condition to be welcomed. Precisely because everyone is free of lawful constraint, the state of nature is a condition of potential conflict, a war of all against all. All individuals in such circumstances, Hobbes argues, have over-whelming practical reason to join any compact or agreement which will put an end to the state of nature, because even those who are strong are vulnerable on some occasions (in sleep or illness for instance) and can never be certain therefore of securing their desires and interests. It is only by making such an agreement, Hobbes thinks, that social peace and order is possible.

The compact likely to be effective, however, is not a matter of conditionally entrusting our rights to a third party, such as Locke's magistrate. Rather, it is based on a recognition of the overriding need for an *absolute* sovereign power, a governing individual (or assembly) who will have the authority to rule absolutely in the interests of peace and order. The individual in the state of nature is driven by desire, and in that state is free to pursue those desires. Perpetual conflict, however, frustrates the satisfaction of these desires, and consequently practical rationality shows that the maximization of desires is to be achieved more effectively under the governance of an absolute sovereign. This is why there is reason for every individual to agree to leave the state of nature.

Conceived in this way, the state of nature is decidedly different to the state that Locke imagines, and so, consequently, is the nature of political authority. For Locke the state of nature is governed by moral principles. It is, he says, a state of liberty, but not of licence. Accordingly, the purpose of forming a political society is not to create law, but to embody these pre-existing moral principles in a body of civil law which the government will then enforce on behalf of its members. By contrast, Hobbes's state of nature *is* a state of licence, and hence a very dangerous one for those who live in it. The purpose of forming a government is to put an end to this condition of danger. It is not a more effective realization of the dictates of morality which Hobbesean people want, but the promotion and protection of their desires and self-chosen purposes. In agreeing to the creation of a political sovereign, they are not consenting to have some federal authority exercise the moral rights they already possess, but accepting a practical necessity by which they completely give up their natural liberty (which for Hobbes is the only sense we can make of 'natural right'), in return for civil or legal rights which will give them a greater chance of securing and protecting their desires and purposes. What motivates people in the state of nature Hobbes imagines is not, as it is in Locke, a concern to see their society run in accordance with the moral law ordained by God, but pure self-interest.

There is, then, quite a marked contrast between these two conceptions of the state of nature, and if we are to employ the domestic analogy outlined in the last chapter, it is obviously important to decide which of these conceptions better fits the world of international affairs. If Hobbes's picture is the more accurate one, then the conduct of international relations is not a matter of applying moral principles to the affairs of nations, but of pursuing national self-interest.

Realism

Many political theorists have thought that Hobbes's *is* the more accurate picture. The first reason they advance for thinking this is that *in reality* international relations are dominated by the pursuit and exercise of power on the part of states with competing national interests, and especially their own security. International society is an '*anarchical* society' (the title of a book by Hedley Bull), in which the law of the jungle is moderated by deals and compromises reached, which are accepted by the parties who make them only as a means to the better security of their interests. This appeal to reality explains why such theorists have been called 'realists'. Among the most famous are the American writers Hans Morgenthau and Reinhold Niebuhr. It simply is not the case, such realists allege, that the pursuit of moral principles enters into the real world of international politics. Some argue that this is because of the intrinsically self-seeking nature of human beings, and others because of the anarchical structure of international relations. But both agree that it is a world in which what matters is the balance of power, not the requirements of justice.

If this is correct, to try to apply abstract moral principles in international negotiations is hopelessly idealistic, and those who attempt to do so are more likely to be duped and cheated than they are to make a significant moral difference to the world. Realism like this about international politics is in fact usually contrasted with idealism in the worst sense of the word, that is, an approach to practical affairs in which the pursuit of moral ideals is self-defeatingly purchased at the cost of effectiveness, where taking a moral stand, or worse, being *seen* to take a moral stand, is of greater concern than making a difference to the course of events.

The realists' first argument, then, is that the real world of *Weltpolitik* is like Hobbes's state of nature, not like Locke's, and that effective action in the international arena requires us to be realistic not moralistic. Between realism and cynicism, of course, there is a somewhat fine line. What passes as a realistic approach to affairs can sometimes be or become a cynical disbelief that anyone is ever to be taken at their word, an automatic assumption that no one ever has anyone's interest at heart except their own. Opponents of realism in international affairs have often taken this view, and accuse realists of possessing a view of reality distorted by cynicism. It sometimes does seem that nations and statesmen act altruistically, and for the realist to claim that in every such case appearances are and must be deceptive looks like an expression of cynicism rather than a solid grasp of reality. It is indeed widely believed that when a world power such as the United States justifies its foreign policy in terms of the defence of freedom, democracy or justice, say, this is often little more than a morally respectable cover for the protection of American economic interests. Certainly the profession of high moral principle on the part of the USSR often cloaked the pursuit of power. For all that, there is an important difference between the claim that professed moral motive and real political motive *may* differ in international relations, and the claim that they *always* do. To discount any and every moral justification of foreign policy in advance and out of hand, is to turn realism about the facts into a cynicism which has ceased to examine the facts at all.

The question – is realism overly cynical? – is hard to settle. The history of international relations is so long and so complex, the numbers of ambassadors, negotiators, agents and heads of state so large, that it is difficult to see how any empirical generalization about actions, plans and motives in world affairs could be formulated and defended adequately. There are just too many contexts and events for any such generalization to encompass successfully. If the dispute between realism and its opponents, therefore, is construed as a disagreement about the facts, there is not much promise of a resolution.

Fortunately, the examination of this important dispute does not have to be left there. Realism can be construed rather more broadly, not as a descriptive account of how international relations *are* conducted, or not only this, but as a prescriptive account of how they *ought* to be conducted. On this interpretation, the realist holds not merely that moral principles generally have little to do with international relations, but more interestingly, that it is *better* if they do *not*. This was the view of Niccolo Machiavelli, the sixteenth-century Florentine political theorist whose name is almost synonymous with a realistically unprincipled approach to public affairs. Machiavelli (1469–1527) is not quite the devil he is sometimes made out to be. In his little book, *The Prince*, the central contention he defends is that political considerations, especially the security of the realm, should always take precedence over moral scruples, and his reasons for thinking so are largely to do with the bad consequences of doing otherwise. Despite the fact that 'Machiavellian' usually implies great cunning and intrigue, Machiavelli's own arguments are not very sophisticated. The principles he advances are rather haphazard and their evidential base largely anecdotal. Still, what Machiavelli represents is a classic version of political realism, for which better reasons can be found than he himself provides.

One plausible argument in defence of *prescriptive* realism begins with the observation that states and nations are not themselves agents. Familiar ways of speaking tend to disguise this fact. We talk of France declaring war, or Britain's foreign aid policy, or the United States signing a convention, but, of course, these things must all be done by human beings who are taken to be the representatives of these countries – heads of state, ambassadors, plenipotentiaries and so on. China or Japan cannot literally pick up a pen and sign an agreement; only their representatives can.

Now, such representatives act on behalf of the countries they represent; they do not act on their own behalf. Their duty is to pursue and promote the interests of the country and people they represent – the national interest – not their own interests. Indeed in so far as representatives, in national as well as international affairs, exploit their position to promote their own, personal interests, they can rightly be accused of corruption. A statesman or politician who uses a public position to advance *national* economic interests is acting honourably; one who uses the same position to advance *personal* economic interest is corrupt.

While it makes perfectly good sense to speak of a country's interests, it is much less clear that it makes sense to speak of its moral principles or beliefs. People, especially politicians, do sometimes use expressions like 'Britain believes . . .' or 'The French people subscribe to . . .' but it is hard to know what warrant they have for doing so. The importance of this observation is as follows: if a country cannot literally have moral principles or beliefs, the only moral principles upon which its representatives could act would be the principles they subscribed to in a personal capacity. *Qua* representatives, however, their personal moral principles should no more influence their public role than should their private interests. To advance a moral cause dear to one's own heart is as much an abuse of power as augmenting one's own bank balance.

If this is correct the prescriptive realist can call upon the important distinction between public role and private capacity in defence of the view that moral considerations should not enter international deliberations. This is because in introducing them, national representatives exceed their proper authority. The single duty and sole right of political representatives in all such circumstances is to pursue the interest of the country which they represent. This excludes moral crusades as much as it excludes personal graft.

It might be replied that it *is* possible for a country to have moral beliefs, if we regard the moral beliefs of a country as those of the majority of its inhabitants. Viewed like this, is it not wholly right and proper for the representatives of that country to act in accordance with the moral beliefs of the majority of its citizens? And can they not reasonably claim to be representing the country's morality rather than their own?

Initially, this seems plausible, but in fact it is not a very convincing rejoinder. To begin with, in many countries, especially in the West, there is a great diversity of moral opinion, and hence no guarantee that any one belief or principle could command the support of the majority. Second, there is widespread moral ignorance and indifference. About the rights and wrongs of, say, nuclear deterrence, foreign aid, humanitarian intervention, very many people have either ill informed opinions or no opinions at all. Third, and in some ways most important, even where there is majority support for some clear moral principle, it can still be objected that to use the coercive power of the state to apply this principle to foreign policy is to trample on the moral freedom of the minority. For example, suppose I believe firmly that charity begins at home and that any available resources of the government should be spent on the homeless and handicapped among my fellow citizens. The majority, by contrast, believes that social justice knows no national boundaries and that there is a greater claim on the part of the world's poorest people. If, on moral grounds, my government distributes some of its tax revenues in the form of foreign aid, I, as a taxpayer, am being forced to contribute to a cause of which I morally disapprove. The question here is not whether I am right or wrong, or even whether there is any justification for imposing upon me the moral opinions of the majority, but whether by declaring the majority's opinion to be that of 'the country' those who are also *my* international representatives are in any sense representing *me*.

The particular example chosen may distort judgement of the general principle, but other examples demonstrate exactly the same point equally well. Suppose that a majority in my country disapproves of homosexuality on moral grounds, whereas I passionately believe in the individual's right to sexual freedom. The invocation of the moral principles of the majority in international relations would justify the expenditure of tax revenues on anti-homosexual campaigns in other countries. Since those tax revenues are raised in small part from me, this means that I am being forced to contribute to the promotion of a cause to which I have deep moral objections. It is, consequently, an infringement of my freedom to be a self-determining moral agent, and to speak of my *country's* opposition to homosexuality simply disguises this important fact.

The relation between political power and the moral beliefs of individuals is not, in fact, any different from that with respect to their religious beliefs, about which agreement is more easily forthcoming. In contrast to the nineteenth century, most people nowadays hold that in foreign policy international representatives should adopt a position of religious neutrality. This is not just a matter of being careful not to take sides, but a matter of respecting individual rights. To invoke the political obedience and use the taxes of minority Christians, for example, in support of a foreign policy which seeks the extension of Islam, is a violation of their religious freedom, and vice versa.

With this argument in mind, realists have a further justification for their insistence that national interest alone should motivate international representatives; to invoke moral principles in international affairs, even when those principles are supported by the majority, is to violate the moral freedom and integrity of some of the citizens represented.

Neutrality and the National Interest

Even if the foregoing argument, elaborated in favour of prescriptive, as opposed to descriptive, realism, is successful, it is not really a defence of the claim that international affairs should be a matter of interests not ethics. At most it is an argument in favour of moral neutrality. It does not show that national interest is the *sole* relevant factor for the representatives of a nation to consider in international negotiations and agreements, only that the introduction of moral considerations violates either the public–private distinction, or the moral liberty of citizens. It follows, or seems to, that the exclusive pursuit of national interest is the best approach to international affairs because it preserves moral neutrality. Two questions now arise, however. Can the national interest be specified independently of moral considerations, and is moral neutralism possible? Let us begin with the first of these questions.

What sorts of things can be said to be in the national interest? Commonly this expression calls two concerns to mind – political security and economic well-being. The arguments about integration, for example, which have dominated European politics in the second half of the twentieth century, can largely be construed along these lines. Those in favour of a highly integrated European Union claim that economic integration, by eliminating all obstacles to trade, increases the economic prosperity of the nations concerned, and that political integration, by preventing the outbreak of war, leads to greater security. Those against the idea of a 'united states of Europe' argue that the integration of disparate economies will exacerbate rather than diminish existing differences, creating rich and poor regions, and that political integration will remove political control to a European level which will reduce the political freedom and security of national government.

We are not here concerned with the validity of these arguments. They serve only to illustrate the kind of factors that are generally thought to be 'in the national interest' and which, accordingly, are held by realists to be the most fitting considerations to bring to international negotiations. If we look more closely, however, we will see that such considerations are not in any interesting sense morally neutral. The pursuit of economic prosperity is a good thing, because it is good for the people who enjoy it. That is to say, an economically prosperous country can provide its people with better diet, health, education, leisure and so on. But the advancement and protection of a better life for people is an intelligible, and familiar, *moral* aim, and statesmen are charged with promoting it for just this reason. Again, why is political security to be valued and war avoided? The answer in part is that this way people are spared pain and suffering, and kept free from oppression and injustice. But once more these are familiar moral ideals. In striving to promote the national interest, therefore, international negotiators are not ignoring moral ideals, but pursuing them.

Of course, it will be said that they pursue these moral aims and ideals only on the part of those they represent, and that consequently it is not their responsibility to consider the moral claims of those who are not of their nation or state. Now these two claims appear to go together, but in fact the implication does not hold. We need to examine the line of thought more closely. If it is agreed that in pursuing the welfare and security of their respective countries international representatives are pursuing moral aims, and hence are morally motivated, an important assumption which realists often invoke has to be modified or even abandoned. This is the assumption that negotiators in the international arena are like individuals in Hobbes's state of nature, essentially egoistic and without moral motivation. This, we have now seen, is not so. It is a mistake to think that pursuit of national interest is on the same level as pursuit of personal interest, because national interest includes the well-being of many and not just of one.

But granted the existence of moral motivation on the part of statesmen, soldiers and so on, granted, that is to say, that we are not dealing here with pure egoism, there is no reason to suppose that the moral claims of others are of absolutely no account. One way of putting this is to say that international agents have *special* but not *exclusive* duties to the countries on whose behalf they act. To appreciate this point consider a parallel with other special relationships, those of family for instance. Someone who is acting on behalf of a family has a special duty to promote the interests and welfare of its members rather than those of the members of other families. I am responsible for seeing that *my* children have enough to eat and are properly clothed, but do not have this special responsibility for yours. But it does not follow from this that your children have no claim whatever on me. There are many things I cannot justifiably do to them, even though I am concerned with the welfare of my children rather than myself – I cannot steal food or clothes from your children to give to mine; I cannot murder or enslave them in the interests of mine. And there may be positive duties towards them too. I cannot justifiably fail to rescue *other* people's children from fire when I could easily do so, just because they are not *my* children.

This parallel, of course, employs the very domestic analogy which has yet to be examined. But the point it serves to illustrate here provides an answer to the second question – about the possibility of moral neutrality. We have seen that there is no bar to including moral aims like the welfare and defence of others under the label 'national interest'. It follows that, contrary to realist conceptions, those charged with pursuing the national interest do not have to be thought of as national egoists, so to speak, public representatives of collective self-interest. They are, and indeed have to be *morally* motivated. That is to say, public representatives are sensitive to altruistic obligations, namely their obligations to other citizens. How else could they represent their interests? However, there is no reason to think that moral sensitivity or motivation stops at political boundaries. Why should it? If other people's welfare is a reason for my pursuing certain courses of action, it does not cease to be a reason just because of their geographical location.

At the same time, what the point about family responsibilities shows is that attributing moral motivation to political representatives does turn them into universal altruists, concerned with the welfare of the global community as a whole rather than the national they represent. They can be regarded as having *special* duties and responsibilities to their own countries while at the same time being regarded as being sensitive to, and hence subject to, at least *some* moral claims on behalf of the citizens of other countries. So, in answer to the two questions with which this section began – can the national interest be specified independently of moral considerations, and is moral neutralism possible? – we can now reply: first, that there is no reason to specify 'the national interest' independently of moral aims and ideals, and that having done so there is no good reason to think all such aims and ideals are neutralized at national borders.

The Domestic Analogy

If the argument of this chapter is sound thus far, the position of the prescriptive realist who wants to exclude ethics from international affairs is unwarranted. But there is still a lingering uncertainty. Statesmen, soldiers, ambassadors and so on, whose special responsibility is to fellow citizens, may have general moral duties to other *people*. But do they have duties to other *countries*? So far we have relied on a parallel – the parallel between the domestic and the international case – which it is now time to examine more closely.

Consider three examples of what would generally be considered morally reprehensible behaviour.

1   A man is standing in a park when fighting breaks out between some children. It is clear to him that a weaker party has been subject to unprovoked attack, possibly with the intent of robbery or subjugation. The bystander is stronger than either of those involved in the fighting, and being relatively impartial and uninvolved, could intervene to good effect, repel the aggressor and thus defend the innocence of the victim and prevent injury on both parts. Yet he limits his intervention to remonstrating with the aggressive child, and, his remonstrations going unheeded, remains on the sidelines and lets violence take its course.

2   Someone who enjoys relatively high levels of power and prosperity knows that these are the result of fraud or violence on the part of ancestors from whom they have been inherited. The dependants of the victims whom his parents or grandparents cheated and exploited live in his neighbourhood, and are rather obviously suffering from the effects of the powerlessness and poverty they have in their turn been bequeathed. His wealth is such that he could do a great deal to alleviate their circumstances without risk of reducing his condition to theirs. Yet his assistance is limited to the rather meagre offerings that are prompted by his not infrequent, but nonetheless sporadic feelings of charity.

3   A woman uses the same streets as people seriously malnourished and sometimes close to starvation. She herself, by contrast, has more than plenty and, indeed, very considerable stores of food. When, from time to time, these stores come close to overflowing, she destroys the surplus food or throws it away. Occasionally, it is true, if her attention is drawn to the plight of the starving more forcibly than usual, or if their situation is exacerbated by additional disease or disaster, she directs some of

the surplus in their direction. But there is nothing systematic about her doing so, and nothing permanent about the improvement or even relief it secures.

There might be different analyses of where precisely, in any of these cases, the fault of the individual lies – personal timidity, indifference, injustice or inhumanity are alternative, not necessarily exclusive, explanations. But although the moral analysis might vary, it is likely that they would all be roundly condemned. In the absence of very special circumstances, most people would have little hesitation in declaring morally wrong the behaviour of the person who, for whatever reason, ignored the misfortunes of the innocent, the disinherited and the starving.

Such moral certainties are relatively rare, and for this reason it is tempting to extend and build upon them. International relations is one area in which this is commonly attempted. People often ask whether the moral dimension of the examples imagined is any different to that which obtains between states where there appear to be exact parallels – states who stand idly, or at least ineffectually by where there is armed aggression by one nation against another, states who ignore the consequential obligations generated by the past deeds of their colonialist ancestors and states that are indifferent to the evident disparity in affluence and poverty between their own citizens and those of other countries.

The parallels *seem* plain enough, and for this reason it is widely believed that an extension from the domestic to the international context preserves the same moral certainties. Consequently, arguments to the contrary, which suggest that the international context makes an important difference, are frequently dismissed as exercises in self-excusing sophistry. There are, as we shall see, important objections to extending the principles of domestic morality in this way, but so widespread is the assumption that the analogy works, we should assume that the burden of proof is on those who wish to draw a distinction between the domestic and the international cases, to show that there really is a difference. This is for two reasons. First, it is an indispensable moral principle, most famously explicated by the philosopher Immanuel Kant (1724–1804) in what is known as the thesis of universalizability, that like cases must, morally, be treated alike. That is to say, if we are to justify treating one case differently from another, in this instance an international case from a domestic one, we have to show that there is a morally relevant difference between the two. On its own, however, this principle is not as powerful as it might appear. Since it does not lay down criteria for what is to count as a 'like' case, some could accept it while consistently denying that domestic and international relationships are alike – states are not persons, after all. So accepting the requirement of universalizability does not logically compel us to accept the domestic analogy for international ethics. Nevertheless, and this is the second reason for thinking that the burden of proof falls on those who would deny the analogy, persuasiveness is no less important in argument than logical validity, and the fact that the domestic cases strike many, perhaps most, people as comparable with the international ones, taken in combination with the universalizability principle, is sufficient to show where the burden of proof lies in real argument.

What is required, then, from anyone who would dispute the extension of these moral certainties, is some demonstration that there really are relevant differences here.

Factual Disanalogy

There are at least two sorts of difference which the opponent of the analogy might seek to demonstrate. The first of these are what we may call *factual* differences. Consider the first example again. In many, and possibly most, international episodes, the relative guilt and innocence of the parties to a war or civil strife is never as clear as that in the imaginary domestic example. In a similar way, the relative military strength and political impartiality of third parties in world politics is rarely, if ever, so clearly realized. Thus it is plausible to argue that in the strife which followed the collapse of the former Yugoslavia, there was aggression on *all* sides, and that military action by Nato or the United Nations was strategically difficult and of uncertain effect. These are, it is true, merely factual differences, but they are of great importance. To accuse the Western powers justly of indifference to international injustice, it must actually be the case that innocent parties are not protected when they could be.

Similarly, in the second example – benefiting from the crimes of ancestors – the facts of the case upon which the analogy rests can be disputed. Indeed, if the moral parallel in the international case is taken to be relations between former colonies and former colonialists, it has in fact been expressly disputed. P. T. Bauer has argued as follows:

> Whatever one thinks of colonialism, it cannot be held responsible for Third World poverty. Some of the most backward countries never were colonies, as for instance, Afghanistan, Tibet, Nepal, Liberia. Ethiopia is perhaps an even more telling example (it was an Italian colony for only six years in its long history). Again, many of the Asian and African colonies progressed very rapidly during colonial rule, much more so than the independent countries in the same area. At present one of the few remaining European colonies is Hong Kong – whose progress and prosperity should be familiar. It is plain that colonial rule has not been the cause of Third World poverty.
>
> Nor is the prosperity of the West the result of colonialism. The most advanced and the richest countries never had colonies, including Switzerland and the Scandinavian countries; and some were colonies of others and were already very prosperous as colonies, as for instance North America and Australasia. (Bauer, 1980, p. 75)

Bauer's rehearsal of familiar facts is sufficiently convincing to raise a serious doubt about moving too quickly from the local to the global context. Certainly, some of the applications of the domestic analogy that have been made (and continue to be made) in this sort of example are too easy, and once again we should note that the facts of the matter are very important from a moral point of view. It is only if currently wealthy nations *are* as a matter of historical fact the beneficiaries of past conquest and exploitation of currently poor ones that there is a moral fault to be remedied.

However, important though factual differences are, their existence is not in itself enough to show the irrelevance of the domestic analogy. This is for two reasons. 'The facts' in this sort of context are often difficult to ascertain because they involve, say, historical records in need of interpretation, complex statistical calculations with imperfect data, or estimates of probable outcomes involving many factors. To rest the case against the domestic analogy on a claim that the facts will always be different in the two kinds of case, is just too ambitious a claim to make.

But a second and more important reason for thinking that factual differences are not enough to show the inapplicability of the analogy is the relative analytical superficiality of this kind of difference. Factual disagreements about complicated political and historical episodes may be difficult to resolve, and on occasions, given imperfect evidence and data, may even be intractable. To acknowledge this, however, is really to leave the central question about the applicability of the domestic analogy in the international context untouched. Relying on factual differences as the only relevant differences between the two cases concedes that *if* the facts *were* as alleged, the moral parallel *would* hold, whereas the crucial question is whether, given that relevant factual similarities do hold, the domestic analogy is a good one at the level of moral concepts. This brings us to the second sort of difference that the opponent of the domestic analogy might seek to demonstrate, namely differences in the moral dimensions of the two contexts.

Moral Disanalogy

In what could such differences consist? One obvious place to start is with moral responsibility. Consider again the first imagined example. The bystander who observes aggressive violence which he could prevent is deemed morally blameworthy for inactivity. It is important to see, however, that his inactivity is unlikely to be completely unmotivated, because there will be a cost to him, however small, attached to intervention. That is to say, no positive act of prevention on his part could be cost free. Even if the effort it takes is minimal, there is always an opportunity cost, the alternative benefits he could derive from the time it takes to intervene.

In the international case, of course, the costs of intervention will certainly be higher. Military action, even diplomatic action, is never undertaken at mere opportunity cost, and this is a significant factual disanalogy. But from the point of view of morality, a more important question is: who bears this cost? In the domestic case, the costs, whatever they are, fall on the bystander, and the point is that morality requires us to accept burdens in order to benefit others, to some degree at any rate. The certainty in the imagined case arises from its being one in which the imagined costs are very low, and the benefit to others very high. If, however, we substitute states for people in the example, there is an added moral dimension: there are now other parties with no counterpart in the domestic case as it was imagined.

Although it is perfectly intelligible to speak of states taking military action, it is not literally true that states engage in fighting; only soldiers do this. Since soldiers are under orders, and in the normal case are not expected to review the reasons for military involvement themselves, a gap opens up between those who would decide to intervene and those who would pay the costs of that intervention. In the domestic case, the bystander himself pays the cost of intervention and we can reasonably hold him to be morally obliged to do so, just because failure in this respect is moral failure. That is, it shows that he has preferred his own benefit or comfort to his obligations to others. But in the international case, it is not the decision taker's own benefit or comfort which is at stake. Consequently, even if the decision is taken on 'moral' grounds, it is *not* a case of accepting moral responsibility in preference to personal comfort. Those who decide on intervention do not make the sacrifice, and those who pay the costs of intervention do so because they are ordered to.

Once the existence of this more complex relationship is noted, we can see that the parallel with the domestic example breaks down. The true parallel would be with someone who, faced with the imagined circumstances in the park, used his greater strength and/or authority to compel someone else, another party, to intervene, and at their cost rather than his. But if this *is* the true parallel, the original moral certainty – that the bystander is morally wrong not to intervene – evaporates once we move from a domestic to a political context.

A similar point can be made about the second example. In the domestic case, the obligation falls on the known descendants of the aggressive exploiter to transfer some of their surplus to the known descendants of the victim. In the international case, the transfer is not between individuals but between states, and once again this introduces an important moral difference. Government to government compensation, we know, is not always raised at the expense of the rich or effectively channelled to the poor. This creates the possibility that the burdens and benefits of compensation do not fall in the right place and hence that wrongs are not in fact rectified and justice is not done. Moreover, even if it were the case that the transfer was from rich to poor, the moral relation of donor to recipient is quite different if the compensation is from state to state rather than individual to individual. Such compensation is produced by governments from taxpayers, not ordered by the courts against the guilty. This means that those who decide to redress ancient wrongs by Congressional votes or Acts of Parliament, bear, at most, a tiny proportion of the cost of doing so. Rather, through their control of the power and authority of the state, they compel others, by means of taxes and so on, to transfer some of their resources to people whom the government deems more deserving. Neither the actions of the legislators nor the taxpayers, consequently, can be praised for the paying of just recompense. It is simply an enforced transfer of resources, and though this may be beneficial and to this degree commendable, it is not the same, morally speaking, as the righting of past injustices.

Once again the parallel with the original domestic example breaks down, importantly with respect to the moral relationships that all three examples are intended to illuminate. The same is true of the third example of the woman who is persuaded to share her food with the starving. The more accurate parallel with states, in such a case, would be with a woman who, confronted by the needs of the poor, compels *others*, who are under her control (her servants or tenants, say) to hand over some of *their* surplus. In such a case, some good may certainly be achieved – the starving are fed at the cost of those less badly off. But it is quite unclear that the woman's moral responsibility has been discharged, or that moral merit attaches to the tenants or servants who have been forced to alleviate the poverty. To put the point succinctly: the moral merits of a Robin Hood (who stole from the rich to give to the poor), and of those whose money he takes, are much less clear than the moral merits of a St Francis (who freely gave away his own considerable wealth). Once again, the moral clarity of the domestic case has disappeared by extending it to an international context.

What is wrong with the analogy in all three cases, is its undefended assumption that individuals and collective entities are to be treated alike as far as moral responsibility is concerned. It has often been said that states have rights on a par with those of individuals. This is indeed a claim from which the domestic analogy gains much of its plausibility. But a more important issue, we have seen, is whether states have moral responsibilities that can be exercised in the way that those of individuals can.

Moral responsibility is not the only significant moral difference arising from the fact that the actions of states are not those of an individual human agent. The example of relieving abject poverty reveals another. There have frequently been drastic famines in parts of Africa when at the same time huge agricultural surpluses have existed in Europe. To many people, these two facts, side by side, are morally obscene. How could Europeans morally justify a failure to transfer them? Here again, the domestic analogy is hard at work. The picture is that of an individual who, being possessed of more than she needs, steadfastly refuses to hand it over to those who have nothing. Yet there are significant differences. To begin with the international case is causally more complex. In transferring resources from country to country, it is not merely relations between givers and given that come into play, but relations between systems of production and distribution. It has been argued for instance, and with good reason, that wholesale transfer of food to famine-stricken areas (leaving aside logistical problems) can have a disastrous effect upon indigenous food production as the impact on demand and hence on price causes the local market to collapse. The involvement of such factors in the context of international assistance not only raises problems about future production, when the emergency relief is ended, but shows that once again, in the international context, there are third parties to be considered. Such state-to-state transfers of relief have effects not only on those who give and who receive, but on food producers who may not be directly involved in the famine. There is a danger, in other words that wealthy Europe generously displays its largesse to moral applause, but at little cost to Europeans and at great cost to local small farmers.

This is not the principal difference, however. It is never literally true that a country is starving, only that large numbers of its people are. As was demonstrated in the catastrophic Ethiopian famine of 1984, it is possible to give 'Ethiopia' assistance and yet fail to give it to starving Ethiopians. By the transfer of resources a country may be better off, its food or financial reserves greatly increased, say. But it does not follow that suffering and hardship is relieved. This depends on what happens within the country, not between countries. In the case of Ethiopia it was not thought possible for foreign governments to transport and distribute food directly on the grounds that this would have been a violation of national sovereignty. As a consequence, much of the aid was ineffectual. Respect for the principle of national sovereignty is an important dimension of international relations. The basis and justification of this principle is a topic for a later chapter. The point to be made here is that it has no counterpart in the domestic analogy and yet alters the moral dimensions by creating a gap between the moral purpose of aid – the relief of suffering – and the action itself – assisting another country.

The distinction between a country and its people is the main reason for the collapse of the domestic analogy, and its moral importance can be illustrated in all three cases, because, extended to the international realm, defence of the innocent, compensation of historic wrongs and relief of poverty cannot but involve third parties. In the domestic cases, moral decency requires that protection, compensation and relief be afforded to those who require them through the actions of the relevant moral agents. We have seen that two features of these cases generate the reasonably certain moral judgements they support. First, the agents in question are specially placed to supply the relevant benefits. Second, the costs attaching to doing so are reasonable and fall only on them. Taken together, it is these two aspects which make their moral responsibility clear. In the international case, by contrast, where states and governments are involved, gaps open up between decision, action and cost, such that scope of obligation and the lines of responsibility are blurred.

It is tempting to avoid the complexity of moral responsibility and restore some plausibility to the analogy by adopting a strictly consequentialist point of view. That is to say, we might focus entirely on the consequences of state action. If there is a reasonable prediction that state to state action will have good consequences, is this not enough to generate an obligation without worrying about the moral merits of those who fulfil it? By taking this approach, it seems, the question of responsibility fades and with it the difficulties it introduces.

The moral significance of the distinction between country and people is not so easily avoided, however. Now a different question arises, one having to do with the identity of the recipients of the beneficial consequences. To fulfil our obligations we must not only do good, but do good to the right people. Take the example of defending a country which has been the victim of an aggressor. Providing such a country with arms, say, may indeed bring an end to much death and destruction, and no doubt this is a good thing. But all wars have their innocent casualties, and launching or assisting a war which ends in peace does not necessarily mean that those originally subject to unprovoked aggression have been given the protection their innocence requires. They may have been the chief casualties, and another or different group of their fellow citizens who did not suffer in the same way may become the beneficiaries of the peace. Nor, for that matter, does the defeat of the aggressor country necessarily mean that those responsible for the original aggression have been punished. The defeat of Iraq in the Gulf War was not the punishment of Saddam Hussein, and those who suffered most from it were, by and large, innocent of aggressive intent towards Kuwait.

The same point may be made about righting historic wrongs. To compensate the Navajo, say, as an ethnic group, need not translate into the compensation of those whose relative poverty can actually be shown to have a particular causal origin. Indeed, given the distance in time, it is unlikely that those who undoubtedly benefit are being recompensed, since those who were injured in the first place are long since dead.

The point to be stressed is this: even if we concentrate on beneficial outcomes we cannot straightforwardly extend the domestic analogy to the international context. Meeting moral obligations in the sorts of case under discussion requires not only that good is done, but that it is done to the right people.

Ethics in the Anarchical Society

We have found reason to doubt the idea that where relative moral certainties prevail in domestic examples, and where on the surface there is an analogy to be drawn with international relations, ethical lessons for international relations can be drawn to good effect. The domestic analogy breaks down, not just because there are, and are always likely to be, important factual differences between domestic and international cases, but because moving to the international context alters the structure of the moral relationships involved. This leaves us with a question. If the domestic analogy will not help us in international ethics, what will?

Part of the reason for rejecting the domestic analogy arises from the fact that when a country acts, those charged with taking its decisions or carrying them out are not properly regarded as moral agents in their own person. Rather, as we saw earlier, they are the occupants of public roles – as rulers, ambassadors, soldiers and so on. This observation suggests that a modification of the first of the original examples might offer some illumination. In this example a man is standing in a park when fighting breaks out between some children. Although he could intervene to good effect, he limits his intervention to remonstrating and, his remon-

strations going unheeded, remains on the sidelines and lets violence take its course. Now an alternative course of action is for
the man, if he is anxious about personal involvement, to call a
police officer. In this case, it is important to note, whether we
regard the man as having fulfilled his obligation or not, the
obligation on the police officer to intervene is of a different kind.
It arises not from principles of individual moral responsibility, but
from his appointed legal and civic duty. It is, we might say, not
merely his duty but his job to intervene.

Extending this amended example from a domestic to a global
context brings us back to the nature of the international order.
The analogy seems inappropriate because it invokes a domestic
legal order that has no international counterpart. The relationship
between intervening forces and the disputants between whom
they intervene, even where those forces have the sanction of an
international body like the United Nations, is not the same as
that which exists between the officers of a legal system and two
parties equally subject to that system. People may speak of UN
forces as international policemen, but this is at best a handy
metaphor, because in the international context, unlike the domestic, there is no sovereign, and hence no duly appointed
police, which is why Hedley Bull describes it as an anarchical
society.

Still, this modification of the original example may provide an
indication of where the argument should go next. As Bull points
out, to say that international society is anarchical is not to say that
it is without order. Nation states, even rival ones, manage to
make agreements which last. Consider, for instance, the remarkable worldwide co-operation which permits an international
postal system, and there is a substantial body of international law
which is adopted, interpreted and applied, and even to a degree
enforced, by international courts of justice. The world of nation
states is anarchical, but it is not Hobbes's state of a perpetual war
of all against all.

There are, however, *some* wars, and while it is striking how
relations between nations can continue even in war (British
manufacturers and traders supplied the French army during the
Napoleonic wars, for instance), war often occasions the break-

down of international law and co-operation. It is in war that the absence of an international sovereign, a world policeman, is most marked. Here even the amended domestic analogy breaks down completely. If we want to articulate ethical principles of truly international relations, however, this can be construed as an advantage, because there is a set of moral principles which were formulated precisely in recognition of the absence of a sovereign power. These are the principles of justice known as the theory of the Just War. The Christian theologians who first formulated these principles believed in the ultimate sovereignty of God, and in the unity of Christendom. But the problem which they sought to deal with was the existence of conflict between Christian sovereigns, between, that is to say, those who recognized the authority of the law of God but not the authority of each other to implement it.

The theory of the Just War is specially interesting in the present context because it is expressly concerned with relations where there is *no* domestic analogy. It involves concepts of justice and injustice where there is no relevant positive law. It therefore represents an important logical possibility – that there are ways of thinking about international relations in terms of right and wrong which go beyond the level of positive law, as Locke's 'Natural Law' does, but do not illicitly extend the principles of personal morality by means of domestic analogies. Of course, the original scope of the theory related to only one area of the relations between states, namely war, and for this reason may be limited. Later chapters will explore the question of how far Just War theory can provide an ethical structure which can be adapted to other relations. At any rate, it is a promising place to begin, and it also introduces the first substantive moral topic – the ethics of war.

Suggestions for further reading

Thomas Hobbes, *Leviathan*, chapters 13–21. A helpful commentary is, F. S. McNeilly, *The Anatomy of Leviathan*.

T. R. Nardin and D. R. Mapel (eds), *Traditions of International Ethics*. A comprehensive set of essays on a wide variety of approaches to international ethics. Essays 4, 5 and 6 will be found specially relevant.

Hans Morgenthau, *Politics Among Nations: The Struggle for Power and Peace*, 2nd edn. A highly influential, and much discussed, elaboration of the realist position.

Peter Singer (ed.), *A Companion to Ethics*, relevant entry: Will Kymlicka, 'The Social Contract Tradition'.

3

War

The theory of the Just War tries to lay down and explain the conditions under which engaging in war can be justified. The attempt to do this, however, presupposes that there *are* some such conditions. It is a presupposition that can be questioned, and there is a longstanding tradition of thought that does question it, namely pacifism. Pacifism, as it will be discussed in this chapter, holds that engaging in war can *never* be justified.

Christian Attitudes to War

While the origins of Just War theory may be traced to ancient Greece and the writings of Plato and Aristotle, pacifism is of largely Christian origin. It seems clear that many if not most early Christians were pacifists. Only a tiny number are recorded as having served in the Roman army, for instance, and the most prominent of the early Christian Fathers, who first forged the elements of Christian moral theology, argued that there was no significant difference between killing on a personal level and killing in war. Both, as they saw it, were cases of homicide.

Although there are familiar passages in the New Testament which pacifists can cite ('Turn the other cheek', for instance), Biblical texts do not altogether sustain a pacifist view. In the first place, they are somewhat scattered, and, in the second, they are open to differing interpretations. So it is not easy to say why the early Christians were strongly pacifist. Some historians have argued that it was antipathy to the Roman army and Roman empire. Partly this had to do with the danger of idolatry; the Roman emperors to whom soldiers swore allegiance were often made, or declared themselves, to be gods, and no Christian could accept an oath that implied an alternative divine authority. Partly it had to do with the fact that until the conversion of the Emperor Constantine, Rome frequently persecuted Christians, and they had every reason therefore to refuse to serve in its army. Other historians have argued that pacifism arose from the early Christians' firm belief in the Second Coming of Christ and the end of the world. Just as anticipation of a speedy end to all things led them to take a rather relaxed attitude to slavery, it also led them to think that there was little point in going to war.

Against both these explanations must be set the facts that Christian pacifism persisted even when the belief in an imminent Second Coming faded, and that it also persisted as Roman persecution died away. This suggests that it sprang from a more directly ethical view about violence and killing. Probably the best explanation of early Christian pacifism is the importance that was attributed to Christ's injunction to 'Love your enemy'. Passages interpreting this as a crucial commandment incompatible with killing can be found in Clement of Alexandria, Tertullian, Cyprian and Justin Martyr, all of whom were powerful influences on the formation of Christian moral theology in its first two centuries or so.

As time passed Christian attitudes broadened, however, and for good reason. Roman rule, which depended so much on the army, brought peace over a wide area and a far higher degree of general lawfulness. Travel both on land and on sea was safer than most people had ever known. Christians, as much as pagans, appreciated and benefited from the relative orderliness of the Roman world, but their acknowledgement of this conflicted somewhat with opposition to arms and the profession of fighting. The tension in Christian attitudes prompted this remark from the pagan critic Celsus: 'If all men were to do the same as you, there would be nothing to prevent the king from being left in utter solitude and desertion and the forces of the empire would fall into the hands of the wildest and most lawless barbarians.' His point in part was this: loving your enemy does not bring about the defeat of lawlessness or the protection of its victims both of which the Christians recognized to be good. And a further point about Christian attitudes is to be inferred from this. It is one thing to follow Christ's injunction towards those who are attacking *me*, quite another to stand by while they attack *someone else*, especially if this is an innocent third party, defenceless widows and orphans for instance.

Some theologians responded to this criticism by arguing that since violence and conflict arise from sinful desires – greed, pride and so on – Christians were indeed engaged in combating evil, at a deeper level, however, and by means of prayer and preaching. Such a response implied that the only and finally effective way of securing peace and order was a wholesale change in the hearts of men and women. Lasting peace would come from the transformation of the world. The strategy of universal redemption, however, takes little account of immediate practicalities. It is what is known as a counsel of perfection, and it was when theologians and churchmen themselves began to doubt this perfectionism that the idea of justified killing in war came to be an important part of Christian thinking.

The major figure associated with the rejection of perfectionism was St Augustine (AD 354–430), Bishop of Hippo in North Africa. Augustine came to the view that the 'City of God' (the title of his major work) would never be brought to completion in this world. Human being are denizens of *two* worlds, the earthly and the heavenly cities, inextricably linked until God brings history to an end. So, since war was an inevitable outcome of the mixed and hence defective character of this world, Christians would sometimes have to engage in it. It was in this belief that he set about formulating the rules by which they would be justified in doing so, building upon the teachings of St Ambrose and others.

Christian attitudes to war broadened still further as the centuries passed. St Augustine died just as the Goths and Vandals from

Northern Europe were finally destroying the Roman empire. These 'barbarians', as the Romans thought of them, brought with them a culture in which fighting and warfare, far from being frowned upon, were hailed as occasions when great bravery, prowess and heroism could be displayed. The Vandals were militarists in the sense that they thought highly of military virtues. Early Christian pacifists (Justin Martyr is a particularly clear example) regarded warfare as an untouchable evil. Augustine's modified view also regarded it as an evil, though sometimes a necessary one in which Christians could justifiably take part. By contrast to both these positions, militarists regarded battle as a positive good.

The North European barbarians did not entirely reject the Christian religion, which by this time had become the official religion of Rome. Many converted to it in fact, but with respect to warfare they changed the religion more than it changed them, for they brought into Christian thinking the idea of a *holy* war, the idea, that is to say, that waging war against infidels and unbelievers could be a positive virtue on the part of Christians. Whereas in the first 150 years after the death of Jesus, there was thought to be an inevitable tension between being a soldier and being a Christian, by the time of the early Middle Ages it was possible to be a Soldier for Christ, and it was this spirit that lay behind the Crusades to the Holy Land.

Thus, three distinct attitudes to war are to be found in Christianity – pacifism, conditional justification and militarism. All of them are represented from quite an early period in its history. Subsequently, ideas about the morality of war lost much of their religious and theological setting, of course, and became ethical attitudes in their own right. There have been secular pacifists, non-religious theories of Just War, and non-Christian, notably Islamic, militarists. The three positions in fact, whether in religious or non-religious versions, encompass nearly all of what could be termed the ethics of war, the topic of this chapter. Though militarism, like imperialism, is a profoundly unfashionable doctrine nowadays, and for this reason little more will be said about it, its continuing importance is this: where the justification of pacifism is under discussion, as in the next section, it is essential to bear in mind that there are *two* alternatives to pacifism, not just one, so that the rejection of militarism does not imply the acceptance of pacifism.

The Case for Pacifism

Militarism sees glory in fighting. It is a view that many societies at many periods have shared. What put an end to its plausibility in the modern period was World War I. We can chart the great change in attitude that this brought about by comparing some of the poetry written at the start of the war with some written at the end, the former filled with exhilaration, the latter with a strong sense of suffering and degradation. To those who joined the war under the inspiration of militarism, the reality proved a grim correction, and led the poet Wilfred Owen, towards the end of the war, to describe the famous military motto *dulce et decorum est pro patria mori* (how sweet and honourable it is to die for one's country) as 'the old lie'.

World War I was the first truly mass war, one which embroiled hundreds of thousands in almost unimaginable suffering. It may be possible to see a measure of glory in the celebrated Charge of the Light Brigade during the Crimean War, say, but impossible to find it in rat-infested trenches filled with the rotting bodies of those destroyed by the impersonal means of shelling and machine gun fire.

If World War I removed any plausibility in the idea that war could be glorious, it confirmed pacifists in their view that war was to be avoided at all costs. For them it simply repeated on a staggering scale what should always have been known, that war is an unmitigated evil, the cause of pain, displacement and death. The point of war, one such commentator remarked, was not to lay down your life for your country, but to force the enemy to lay down his life for his.

That war, and especially modern warfare, is a great evil is not to be denied. But to hold that under no circumstances whatever can it justifiably be engaged in we have to show that it is an *absolute* evil, that is, one without any redeeming features. In what could such a demonstration consist? An obvious answer is to detail the suffering and death it causes. But not all wars are waged for aggressive purposes. Some are defensive. To fend off an invading army by means of war may save lives as well as take them. What if we could show that the suffering and death war causes is on some occasions less than that which it prevents? When this is true, if ever it is, we can agree that waging war is an evil, but see ourselves under an obligation to prefer the lesser of two evils. To take this view is to share, not to dispute, the pacifist's claim that that which makes war evil – death and suffering – is to be avoided or averted, because in so far as waging war minimizes these things, it can be regarded as resistance to evil, not the promotion of it. In short, it is *just* war.

There are at least three responses the pacifist might make. The first is to claim that 'two wrongs don't make a right'. This principle, let us agree, is both correct and important. But to invoke it here begs the question against the proponent of the Just War: aggressive war is a wrong (both sides agree), but it does not follow that defensive war is. To wage a defensive war, therefore, is to commit a wrong only if all war is wrong, which is what the pacifist still has to show. To condemn a defensive war on the grounds that it is a 'wrong' is to presuppose that the pacifist is right, and this is just what is under dispute.

A second response holds that it is always wrong to kill and since war, even defensive war, involves killing, it is always wrong to wage war. Here we need to ask what is wrong with killing. This seems an odd question, but only because the answer to it is so obvious. Killing is wrong because it causes death, and (leaving aside some very special cases) death is a bad thing. But if death is a bad thing, it seems to follow that more of it is worse than less of it, so that if going to war could *reduce* the number of deaths, it would be better to *go* to war than to refuse to do so. Again the pacifist seems to be without a foundation for an absolute ban on war.

This brings us to the third possible response, namely, that war can *never* minimize death. In assessing this response it is important to see that we have moved from the level of the moral to the

level of the empirical, from principle to fact. The claim that war
can never minimize death is a claim about the facts, not about
right and wrong. Consider again the contention that killing is
always wrong. There are familiar cases in which a terrorist, say,
is threatening to kill a number of hostages. To kill the terrorist is
to save the hostages. If death is bad, fewer deaths is better, in
which case it seems that we are justified in killing the terrorist.
Of course, no one need deny that to save the hostages *without*
killing the terrorist would be even better, but it is a factual or
empirical question whether this is possible, and sometimes it is
not. Now extending this line of reasoning to war, we can see that
pacifism needs to hold either that there is always a peaceful
alternative (a view Tolstoy, the great Russian novelist, seems to
have held), or that the number of deaths will always be greater if
two sides go to war. Both claims are guilty of asserting factual
claims in advance of the evidence. And the evidence seems to
count against them. On the one hand there can be, and have
been, limited defensive wars. On the other hand, the ravages of
aggressors can know no bounds unless checked by military defeat.
There is every reason to think that the number of victims of the
Holocaust, huge though it was, would have been even greater if
the Allies had not gone to war against Hitler.

It is important to see that this argument against pacifism,
unlike militarism, shares the objection to killing in war. It claims
only that a lesser evil is better than a greater, and that waging war
can, on occasions, be the lesser evil. Pacifists can, of course, assert
that since killing is an evil, their principles will not let them kill.
This is the position taken by those known as conscientious
objectors. In World War I conscientious objectors were held in
contempt, ridiculed, and even imprisoned as traitors. In World
War II they were less badly treated, though they still tended to be
defamed with insinuations of cowardice. In the Vietnam War
many conscientious objectors were indiscriminately lumped together with 'draft dodgers'.

So harsh and unpleasant were these reactions, that it is in fact
hard to make and maintain an accurate ethical estimate of conscientious objection. Patriotic fervour motivated many of those
who went to war in 1914, and consequently many conscientious
objectors can be seen as justifiably refusing to have anything to

do with an orgy of militarism. The accusation of cowardice may have been appropriate for a few, but given the opprobrium and severe treatment they received, the courage of many conscientious objectors in the face of such a social onslaught was both remarkable and admirable.

In examining the case for pacifism, however, the conscientious objectors' refusal to join the rush to war is not of the greatest interest, because, as we have seen, it is possible to reject pacifism without embracing militarism. More significant, therefore, is the position of those who, believing that killing is wrong, refused to suspend or sacrifice their moral principles. Such strength of will and moral conscience is in many ways admirable, and is now generally admired. But we have to ask what, from an ethical point of view, this position ultimately implies. If and when it is the case that by killing they could reduce the total number of deaths, the refusal to do so can only mean that conscientious objectors would prefer to remain untainted by evil than to save lives. Such a view, which is rarely if ever expressly espoused, amounts to what some philosophers have called 'moral self-indulgence'; that is to say, one's own moral rectitude is more important than the lives and well-being of others. This is a hard conclusion to draw, but though conscientious objectors may certainly pay a price for following the dictates of their conscience (as in the two world wars) so too do any casualties of war whose lives or liberty they might have prevented.

Pacifism as an absolute ban on waging war, then, seems to be without adequate foundation. For the sake of the argument, the pacifist's opponent has been taken to agree that war is an evil. But the strongest, non-militarist, opposition to pacifism claims more than this, that waging war can be positively justified. This is the contention we need to examine next.

Just Wars

While militarists hold that waging war can be a positive good, those who have argued that there can be just wars share the pacifist's belief that the ideal world is one of perpetual peace (the title of an early essay on international ethics by the great philosopher, Immanuel Kant). It was the desirability of peace which had prompted Plato two millennia before to make the first move in what eventually became a full-blown theory of the Just War.

Plato's political world was composed of the Greek city states – Athens, Sparta, Thebes, Corinth and so on. Although just one of these cities tended to dominate the others in turn, by and large they were of equal strength and standing and when war broke out between them this was generally to everyone's detriment. For this reason peace between them was the best condition. But precisely because this was so, Plato saw that a war could be justified whenever it was the best means of *restoring* peace. In short, it was possible to fight a war in a just cause.

That a just war must be fought in a just cause became the first principle of what is known as Just War theory, elaborated at length for the first time by St Augustine. Augustine held, with Plato, that this just cause was the restoration of peace.

> War should be waged only as a necessity and waged only that through it God may deliver men from that necessity and preserve them in peace. For peace is not to be sought in order to kindle war, but war is to be waged in order to obtain peace. Therefore even in the course of war you should cherish the spirit of a peace maker. (Augustine *Epist* 189)

To the restoration of peace, however, Augustine added other possible just causes, avenging injuries for instance. He also took up and amended, from Roman rules of war, not merely principles relating to the necessary aims or purposes of a just war, but principles regulating the way in which it was conducted. This expansion of the theory of justification, both by Augustine and by others, has led to a certain flexibility of interpretation; some variation is possible in setting out just what the principles of the just war are. But in general, as we know it today, the theory has eight major principles, divided into two sets – those known as *ad bellum* principles, i.e. governing the justice of resorting to war, and those known as *in bello* principles, i.e. governing the conduct of the war. These can be stated as follows.

Ad Bellum principles

1 The war must be undertaken and waged exclusively by the leaders of the state.
2 The war must be fought in a just cause.
3 Recourse to war must be a last resort.
4 There should be a formal declaration of war.
5 Those engaging in war must have a reasonable hope of success.
6 The evil and damage which the war entails must be judged proportionate to the injustice which occasions it.

In Bello principles

7 Actions taken in war must be proportionate to their objective.
8 Non-combatants must be immune from attack.

Although these principles are generally known as the *theory* of the Just War, they do not in themselves explain what makes a war just. As they stand, in fact, they simply state criteria, without explanation or justification. Augustine, of course, offered a defence of them, as did the other Christian theologians and moralists who contributed to their elaboration. Their explanations rely chiefly on two elements: first, Biblical texts, and in particular with Jesus' Sermon on the Mount; and second, the idea of a natural law which transcends and has authority over the human laws that individual states may make. Anyone who does not accept the authority of the Bible is unlikely to be persuaded by the first of these, so to appeal to the widest audience, we have to deploy (and make sense of) the idea of natural law alone.

Natural Law

We have already encountered the concept of *natural* law in Locke's version of the state of nature. According to Locke, as we saw, though there is in the state of nature no *civil* law, our actions there are still subject to the 'Law of Nature'. This claim about a natural moral law is best understood as a way of saying that, in the absence of civil authorities, it is still possible for us to commit wrongs against others, or to have right on our side. The ultimate source and authority of the Law of Nature, for Locke, is God, but this does not mean, even for Locke, that it rests directly on the authoritative text of the Bible. This is because our knowledge of the natural law is not dependent on special revelation, but on the use of reason. Through the use of reason, Locke says, natural law is 'plain and intelligible to all men'. The problem he sees is that bias and ignorance get in the way of people agreeing upon what it is. The result is that 'there wants an *established*, settled, known law, and allowed by common consent to be the Standard of Right and Wrong, and the common measure to decide all Controversies between them', and it is from this 'want' that political society and civil law emerge.

Locke's conception of the natural law is not significantly different to that which Augustine invokes. Nowadays it is a conception which has fallen largely into disuse, partly because of the theological background from which it sprang. But despite the old fashioned sound of 'Law of Nature' (except of course its use in the quite different context of physical science), elements of this way of thinking remain at work in moral arguments. Anyone who appeals to the idea of 'natural rights', for example, is making use of this conception, because the term 'natural' right implies a right that we have by the nature of things and not because we have been granted it by some legal system. When people speak of states violating the natural, human or moral rights of individuals (the variety in terminology is not specially significant), they are effectively appealing to the very same idea that Augustine and Locke invoked.

'Natural rights' are one residual element of natural law theory. So too is 'natural justice'. It is not uncommon for the outcome of a legal hearing to be affected by the dictates of natural justice. These include the following principles: that the accused is entitled to a hearing; that no one should be judge in his or her own cause; that the innocent ought not to be punished. Principles such as these are not *legal* principles in the strict sense, for they are not to be found amongst the laws and statutes which have been passed by state legislatures. They are rather, principles of justice and fairness which transcend any particular legal system. They are principles which all legal systems are expected to respect if they are to be called systems of *justice* and not merely systems of law.

With the concepts of natural rights and natural justice in mind, then, and remembering that the theological underpinnings of natural law theory are not directly invoked by it, we can make sense of the *idea* of natural law on which the theory of the Just War rests. The real problem lies in its application.

Justice *Ad Bellum*

Augustine supposed that in any war only one party could have right on its side. His primary concern was to justify participation by Christians in the defence of the Roman empire against the barbarians and he assumed, perhaps correctly, that in this conflict Rome was in the right and the barbarians in the wrong. Whatever the truth about this particular case, it is much less evident that as a general rule only one side in a war could be fighting a just cause. But the difficulty goes deeper than this. Two sides can have competing conceptions of what *counts* as a just cause, and who then is to say which of them is correct? This possibility of deep dispute is one of the reasons that makes Hobbes think the state of nature is a war of all against all. It need not be that people in the state of nature have *no* idea of justice and injustice, but that they have *competing* ideas, and consequently, in the absence of an absolute sovereign to lay down the law and enforce it, the appeal to justice secures nothing.

There seems then to be a great weakness in Just War theory. Everyone could agree with the principle that a just war must be in a just cause, but if they then disagree about what is to count as a just cause, their agreement on the principle counts for very little. Many contemporary wars have been launched, not for economic gain, but in the name of just liberation from servitude and sometimes slavery. Aristotle thought that a war *against* rebellious slaves was a war in a just cause, because by trying to throw off their slavery, slaves were threatening the natural order. No one, or almost no one, would think this nowadays, of course, but it still illustrates that it is possible for the just causes to which appeal is made to be diametrically opposed. A more modern, and more striking example, is the Arab-Israeli War of 1967. If conceptions of justice can themselves be sources of conflict, the second principle of the theory cuts no ice; it allows wars for almost any and every purpose. This is why many people have thought that Just War theory fails almost before it has begun.

Something similar could be said about principle 6, proportionality. That the successful outcome of a war should be of greater value than the cost of the war itself, is a principle on which people might agree, while disagreeing about the relative worth of the values in question. How many lives is national liberation worth, for instance? This is a question about which people profoundly disagree. To some, the political freedom of their ethnic group is worth many lives; to others it is not worth any.

To reject the principles of the just cause and proportionality, and with them the whole of Just War theory on these grounds, however, is too quick a response to the difficulty. To begin with, as Locke observes, people can be biased and ignorant in their interpretation of justice, and this includes both the interpretation of the conception of justice to which they themselves subscribe, and their estimate of relative values. This possibility widens the scope of criticism in terms of the principle of the just cause, even allowing for varying conceptions of justice. For example, many American citizens who criticized their government over the Vietnam War did not dispute the values of freedom and democracy or the justice of protecting them by means of arms. They denied that these values were the real inspiration of US policy or the guiding principles of the prosecution of the war, and if their claims were true, this was effective criticism in Just War terms.

A reply of the same sort can be made on behalf of the principle of proportionality. It is true that people can differ significantly in their estimates of the relative value of the end and the cost of achieving it. But it is also true that they can get blinded to the realities of the situation and think, contrary to their own principles, that any price is worth paying. Countries have gone to war over tiny scraps of worthless land, for instance, and it is not difficult to show in such cases that no one really regards the prize as worth the sacrifice.

But more importantly, doubts about either of these principles are not sufficient to call the whole theory into doubt, because the principles are relatively free-standing. For going to war to be just, each of the *ad bellum* principles must be satisfied independently. We might have doubts about the applicability of the just cause principle, or the principle of proportionality, and yet be clear that other principles were not satisfied. Take for instance the principle of reasonable prospect of success. The rationale behind this principle is that it is wrong to initiate all the destruction and hardship of a war if the intended purpose is most unlikely to be realized. To cause pointless suffering is wrong, and the suffering *is* pointless if the probability of success is low enough. We might disagree with the conception of a just cause which some state espoused, but set this disagreement aside, while arguing that the chances of successfully accomplishing it were too low to warrant the waging of war. Of course, judgements of probability can be difficult to make, and matters of serious disagreement, but two points are worth making. First, they are empirical not moral judgements, so moral disagreement is not a factor here as it is in the just cause principle. Second, although there are disputable cases, there can also be clear cases. Sometimes, often perhaps, judgements of probability are reasonably easy to make. Interestingly, this principle is morally quite powerful. It implies, for example, that heroic wars of resistance with no chance of success are morally wrong. Contrary to popular opinion, only a discredited militarism can justify these.

Other *ad bellum* principles are even easier to apply. The principles that war can only be justly declared by the leaders of the state, and that there must be a formal declaration of war, immediately rule out wars of insurrection and pre-emptive strikes. Unfortunately, this very ease of application raises other difficulties. Their implication is clear, but not obviously correct. Is it true that all wars of insurrection are unjustified? What about a popular revolt against a tyrannical regime? Again, are there no circumstances in which it would be right to make a pre-emptive strike? What about the case in which unwarranted aggression can be forestalled and conflict minimized by attacking first and without warning?

These are important and telling questions. But just as we should not dismiss the whole theory of the Just War because its principles are difficult to apply, so we should not dismiss it because their application conflicts with our unreflective judgements about the rightness and wrongness of war. For after all, if the principles are sound, these unreflective judgements are unsound. We need, therefore, to look, not just at the principles, but the thinking that underlies them.

Force and Violence

Pacifists object to the use of force of arms because it causes pain, death and damage. Sometimes pacifism is for this reason described as absolute opposition to violence. Yet there is an important distinction to be made between force and violence. Force and violence usually have this in common; they involve the infliction of physical pain and injury. This is why people often fail to distinguish them. Force, however, is the *constrained* and violence the *unconstrained* infliction of pain and destruction. It is important to understand what this means. Force, we might say, is violence limited by purpose. Violence proper knows no such bounds. A burglar, for instance, may damage a building by forcing an entry, whereas the damage a vandal does, even if it comes to just the same amount, is pure violence. So too with injury to human beings. I might break your arm while forcing you into an ambulance; this is not the same as breaking your arm in a common assault.

The moral importance of the distinction between force and violence shows itself in the different relation of the two to injury. If my intention is to force you to do something, the threat of violence may be sufficient to make you concur. If it is, I have no reason to inflict that violence; it is pointless from the perspective of my purpose. This shows that coercive force relies on the *possibility*, not the *actuality* of violence. In the case of violence pure and simple, by contrast, no such discrimination makes sense. If I wish to use force, the threat of violence may be enough; if I wish to be violent, the *threat* of violence is not enough.

Just War theorists, in common with most natural law theorists, take it for granted that violence *as such* is an evil. Now, whereas pacifists conclude from this that violence is never justified, natural law theorists hold that violence can be justified as *force*. This justification has two parts, the first of which arises from the *purposefulness* of force. Force is the threat or use of violence to some end. This condition constrains the violence in two ways: (1) violence is never justified if the threat of violence would be sufficient; (2) only such violence as is needed for the purpose in view can be justified − anything in excess of this is unjustifiable.

These conditions on their own, however, are insufficient to justify the use or even threat of violence, as can easily be seen from the fact that armed robbery can satisfy them both. We need to add therefore that the use of force is *legitimate*, and this constrains it in two further ways: (3) the end for which the force is just must be a rightful one; and (4) the person using or authorizing the force must be the person entitled to do so. So, for instance, suppose a woman takes a new born baby meaning only to love and care for it. The baby's natural mother, who also wishes to love and care for it, is entitled to use or recruit force to retrieve it. Even though in this case the first woman's motives are good, the mother has right on her side. But the mother, however angry she may feel, is not entitled to use force if the threat of it would be sufficient, and she is not entitled to employ more force than is strictly necessary to accomplish the return of the baby.

To regard these as *natural* laws is to think of them as fundamental moral principles which hold irrespective of what the civil law may say, or even whether there is any civil law at all. Now, as we have seen, it is a feature of international relations that there is no one sovereign to whom disputants are subject. It is in this respect that the international order is a sort of state of nature. Natural law theory, from which Just War theory is derived, holds however, that the absence of a sovereign does not leave us in a moral vacuum. The laws of natural justice and right can be applied here also, and indeed, given what has been said about force and violence, it is easy enough to see how some of the principles of the Just War are derived. From condition (1) listed above we can see why war should be a last resort. From condition (2) the principle of proportionality follows. From condition (3) we have the principle of the just cause and from condition (4) the restriction that a war can only be declared by the sovereign.

This last principle is the one which is brought into question by the possibility of a justified war of insurrection, that is, a war declared not *by* but *against* the sovereign. This need not be regarded as a major difficulty for Just War theory, however, and most Just War theorists have also believed in justified rebellion. The principle which restricts the right to wage war to sovereigns is based upon two ideas. Wars are fought between armies, armies are corporately organized entities; they are not merely collections of like-motivated individuals, but presuppose an authoritative structure. Now in so far as the declaration of war is the action of one country against another, the supreme authority is the head of state and it is the head of state therefore who alone can legitimize the resort to arms. Civil strife arises where the authority of the sovereign itself is in dispute. Traditionally, Just War theorists have held that by gross abuse of position, a government or head of state can forfeit the authority which makes it sovereign. In such circumstances, however, it does not follow that anyone is entitled to take up arms. There must be some measure of authority — widespread popular consent, for example — which legitimizes the position of the party declaring war. It is not enough for some dissident group, such as the IRA, for instance, simply to pronounce its own campaigns of violence as a 'war'.

In this way, the principles of the Just War can be qualified or amended without losing their force. The theory of the Just War, in fact, remains a plausible, sustained and sophisticated attempt to regulate the conduct of international affairs by ethical principles, in the most demanding and difficult context, violent conflict. From what has been said, however, it should be clear that Just

War theory is a large and complex topic and that it has only been possible to indicate a few of the areas of discussion which its proper consideration requires us to explore. But before we leave it, something must be said about the second, much shorter, list of principles.

Justice *In Bello*

The principles discussed up to this point have all concerned the justice of resorting to war. The second set concerns justice in the conduct of any war resorted to. Augustine saw clearly that it was not enough to have justice on your side in going to war; it must also be carried on in the right way. A war might be justly begun, but fought in a manner that made it unjust.

The *in bello* principles are two. One of these is a repetition of the requirement of proportionality. This principle is not always listed for a second time because its rationale remains the same. It is worth pointing out, nonetheless, that if justice is to be preserved, proportionality applies as much to the strategic and tactical objectives adopted in war as to the prosecution of the war as a whole. Still, when it comes to the conduct of war, it is the principle of non-combatant immunity that has generated most philosophical discussion.

It is best to begin with a consideration of the rationale of the principle. Let us take the relatively simple case where one country (A) is subject to the unwarranted aggression of another country (B), and let us assume, reasonably, that there is no serious dispute about the right to resort to war as an act of defence. The basis of A's right is the threat presented by B. Now given that B is a threat to A, it is, nonetheless, the case that not every member of B is a threat to the members of A; only actual combatants are. Since the basis of A's right is the threat it faces, it follows that there is no right where there is no threat, and hence no right against non-threatening members of B, and from this we can conclude that non-combatants cannot justifiably be attacked by the armies of A.

So much seems clear enough. What is not so clear is the precise definition of 'combatant'. In philosophical discussions of this issue the commonest test case is that of munition workers. Soldiers without arms are no threat, and they cannot have arms unless someone makes them. The people who make them, however, may not be the same people as those who use them. It seems a simple and justifiable defensive move to seek to disarm the enemy's combatants. One way of doing this is to destroy their capacity to manufacture arms, and one way of doing *this*, is to bomb munitions factories. But bombing munitions factories kills civilians not soldiers, namely civilians employed in the manufacture of weapons. How then is the principle of non-combatant immunity to be defended? If we hold to the principle, it seems that we deprive country A of a practical and effective means of defence. If we allow the destruction of munitions factories, and with it the killing of civilians, we permit the killing of civilians, and thus abandon the principle.

It is tempting to mount a defence by making an exception of civilians who manufacture arms for the war effort. The problem is that it is difficult to restrict the exception to this one case. Soldiers cannot fight effectively if they are not fed, transported, provided with clothing, communications and a whole host of other necessities. Any weakening of the principle of non-combatant immunity which excepts munition workers on the grounds of their contribution to the war effort can soon be extended to farmers, drivers, clerks, and almost any other category of employment. Some critics, notably military commanders, have even argued that since the effectiveness of an army depends upon the morale of the country as a whole it is legitimate to attack targets which will have the effect of demoralizing the civilian population at large. Such was the reasoning behind the notorious Allied bombing (during World War II) of the German city of Dresden, which had no strategic value.

It seems then that the principle of non-combatant immunity is worthless. Interpreted narrowly it is impracticable; interpreted broadly there is no one it excludes, and hence no one it protects. Once more however, rejection of the principle on these grounds would be too swift. Consider the division between combatant and non-combatant from the other side, as it were. There are at least some members of B who pose no threat whatever to A — new-born infants, the mentally handicapped, the senile, for example. Nothing done or intended by such people could properly be said to threaten A, and consequently they cannot be justly attacked. It may, nevertheless, be true, that if they were attacked this would contribute to the demoralization of friends and family amongst the armed forces of B. Even so, this does not alter their innocence. The connection between what they are or do on the one hand and the effectiveness of the army on the other is purely causal and entirely passive. New-born infants do not get themselves born, or generate feelings of attachment in others, *in order* to bolster other people's sense of well-being, even though it is true that they may contribute causally to that sense. The mentally handicapped do not belong to families or show great affection for others *in order* to boost their morale, though the fact that they do may actually boost morale. In this respect both groups are in a different position to munitions workers. Munitions workers do produce weapons in order that armies may use them. What other purpose could there be for them, after all?

Once we have grasped this important distinction between intentional action and causal contribution, we can see that there *is* a relevant difference between munitions workers and other groups, and hence a difference between combatants and non-combatants. Combatants are those people the purpose of whose activity is to contribute to the threat; non-combatants are those people who do not actively contribute in this sense, though they may constitute part of a relevant causal chain. To deny this distinction is in effect to deny the idea of intentional agency altogether, for if causal contribution is enough then the horses of enemy cavalry are themselves enemies, despite the fact that they are not intentionally engaged in war at all, but merely used.

The basis of the non-combatant–combatant distinction is the contention that *not* all is fair in war. To reject it, or some similar principle, is in effect to deny that there are any moral constraints at all, that anything that is done in the course of fighting a war is justified if it is effective. Such a position either takes us back to the 'realism' discussed in chapter 2, or appeals to a pure morality of consequence according to which the end always justifies the means. The first of these has been dealt with, the second will be discussed at length in the next chapter. For the moment we may conclude that the important *in bello* principle of the immunity of non-combatants has emerged unscathed from the discussion so far. Before leaving it, however, there are two more points to be considered.

First, it is true that just where the line is to be drawn between combatant and non-combatant is in many cases obscure. For example, farmers who grow the food an army eats need not grow the food for the army. There are many historical instances in which food supplies have simply been commandeered. There are others where the farmers would have grown the food anyway, and would just as happily sell it to other purchasers. There are still other cases, however, in which a 'land army' has been created precisely in order to sustain or increase food production for military purposes. Are agricultural workers non-combatants in the first two cases, but not in the third? My own inclination is to say 'yes', but it has to be agreed that there are reasons in support of varying points of view. In bringing forward this difficulty over the application of the principle, however, we are not pointing to a special difficulty in Just War theory. Almost any moral principle will admit of varying interpretation in its application. For instance, borrowing a book is morally permissible, stealing it is not. But how long may I keep a book I have borrowed before I can be said to have stolen it? Or to take another example: there is nothing wrong with target shooting, but I may not endanger life. How high does the probability of hitting a passing stranger have to be before my shooting at targets moves from the innocent to the reprehensible?

The second, more important difficulty which the principle of the immunity of non-combatants faces is the possibility of casualties. It is easy to secure general agreement that while bombing a military base may be morally acceptable, bombing a children's hospital is certainly not. However, what of the case where the military base is not far from the hospital, and there is a reasonable likelihood that bombs sufficient to destroy it will affect the hospital also. Are we justified in bombing the military base, knowing that there will probably be child casualties?

The Doctrine of Double Effect

In response to this sort of problem some philosophers have appealed to what is called 'the doctrine of double effect' (DDE). This principle states that it is permissible to perform an action even if it has foreseen bad consequential side-effects, provided that these consequences are unintended. Most of us will agree that we cannot be held responsible for wholly unforeseen consequences of our actions. The DDE goes further. It holds that we are not responsible for *foreseen* consequences, if they are unintended. What is the mark of unintended consequences? The answer lies in what is called 'the satisfaction conditions' of our action. If the intention would be satisfied without the foreseeable consequences happening, those consequences are unintended. So, to return to the example with which we began, the unhappy consequence of killing children in the nearby hospital is a foreseen but unintended consequence for which we are not responsible, if our intention (to destroy the military base) is satisfied without their dying. That is to say, in the event that no children are killed, the action we intend to perform is in no way thwarted. In this respect, we can contrast the death of children in this case with one which results from a general policy of demoralizing the enemy. In this second case, the death of children (and other such parties) is a constituent part of the policy and not merely a side consequence.

Does the DDE rescue the principle of non-combatant immunity? In examining this question an initial point is worth making at the outset. The DDE is not an integral part of the theory of the Just War. It is a general moral principle which can be (and has been) invoked in very different cases. Medical ethicists often deploy it in certain cases of abortion and euthanasia. A doctor may undertake a procedure which can be predicted to result in the death of a foetus, for example, if the intention is not to bring about the death of the foetus, but to save the life of the mother. Should the foetus survive as well as the mother, there is cause for rejoicing. The case is therefore morally different, they argue, from the act of abortion properly so called which, since the intention is to terminate the pregnancy, fails if the foetus survives. What this sort of example shows is that we should not expect Just War theory to be, as it were, sufficient unto itself. Although it is concerned exclusively with war, it inevitably relies on a wider framework of moral principles, just as medical ethics and business ethics do.

Still, waging war is a specially nasty business because of its scale and, especially where bombing and shelling are involved, any ethics of war must give some account of side-effects. For this reason, it is important to ask whether the principle of non-combatant immunity can be supplemented by the DDE to good effect, and this means looking critically at the DDE.

Two principal objections have been brought against it. The first is that it is too liberal to serve a useful purpose. That is to say, the DDE is too easily satisfied. Consider these examples, one rather odd, the other unfortunately familiar. I park my car at the kerbside and kill a dog that is lying there. I claim that the death of the dog is a foreseen but unintended consequence of my wholly innocent intention to park my car. Had the dog moved and not been killed, my intention would have been fully satisfied. Or, a terrorist is holding hostages and threatening to kill them if the government does not give into his demand for the release of some comrades. When his demands are not met, he shoots a hostage, and claims that the death is a foreseen but unintended consequence. His intention is to release his comrades, and if this can be accomplished without the death of a hostage, so much the better. In both cases, it seems, the reasoning fits the doctrine of double effect, but if so, the doctrine justifies any kind of wickedness.

The answer to this objection lies in rehearsing the earlier point, that in deploying any moral principle we must bear in mind that it is not to be employed on its own. Leaving aside the question of sincerity of intention, which might be questioned in both these examples, we may say, first, that a proper concern with moral responsibility rules out callous indifference to all but the pursuit of intention. Our intentions, even if good, have to be pursued in the awareness of the best way of fulfilling them. This is why, returning to the original military example, even if the DDE works, there is a duty to minimize the number of children put at risk. Second, although intention is morally important, there are means we cannot properly take to carry them out. From the fact that my intention is innocent, or justifiable, it does not follow that I can take any means to its fulfilment. By appealing to these additional moral principles we can deal adequately with both counter-examples.

The second objection that is commonly brought against the DDE is rather more radical. This relies on the idea that I am responsible for the consequences of my actions. Though it may be true that I cannot be blamed for consequences of which I could know nothing, I am responsible for any bad thing I do knowingly. From this point of view, those who order the bombing of the military base, kill children, and do so knowingly. If killing children is a bad thing, which all must agree or there would be no question of justification, then they knowingly do wrong, and any principle which shows to the contrary is casuistry, an attempt to forge an artificial distance between my actions and their outcome.

A first response to this objection would be that though knowingly doing a bad thing is bad, intentionally doing a bad thing is worse. The very possibility of foreseen but unintended consequences shows that knowing and intending the consequences of our actions are different things. It is a distinction we employ all the time. I may know that alcohol will adversely affect my driving, and having drunk too much have an accident in which someone is injured. However bad this may be, it is to be contrasted, from a moral point of view, from intentionally running someone down in my car.

But is it? This is, in fact, precisely what is under dispute. In either case the result of my action is injury, and for those to whom consequences are all that matter, there is no relevant difference between the two. There is an injured person in the

world where there was not before, and this is something I have
brought about. The objection to the DDE that we have now
encountered is radical in the sense that it challenges something
built into the heart of the doctrine – the moral relevance of
intention. Those who question the moral relevance of intention
on the grounds that all that matters, morally speaking, are the
consequences of actions are known, for obvious reasons, as
consequentialists. Consequentialism is an ethical theory that has
lurked in the background of a good deal of the discussion so far.
The objection to the DDE that we are now considering makes
it appropriate to examine it more directly. In doing so, we can
usefully extend the discussion to another important topic in the
ethics of warfare – the use of nuclear weapons. This is the topic
of the next chapter.

Suggestions for further reading

Roland H. Bainton, *Christian Attitudes toward War and Peace*. A comprehensive and highly informative survey.

Terry Nardin, *Law, Morality and the Relations of States*. Specially useful
on natural law, though its concerns are wider than the ethics of war.

Peter Singer (ed.), *A Companion to Ethics*, relevant entries: Stephen
Buckle, 'Natural Law'; Jeff McMahan, 'War and Peace'.

Jenny Teichman, *Pacifism and the Just War*. A short and readable book,
though the issues are not dealt with in any great depth.

Michael Walzer, *Just and Unjust Wars*. A very wide-ranging treatment
of ethics and the use of arms, with many historical illustrations,
covering the topics of this and the next three chapters.

4

The World of Nuclear Weapons

The Argument So Far

Pacifism is the view that it is always wrong to wage war. An analysis of the case for pacifism revealed no solid basis for this absolute ban. Militarism, in sharp contrast, is the view that there is positive merit in waging war. This is a view which has figured prominently in the moral attitudes of many times and places, but though it would be interesting to locate the fault in militarism precisely, it is so unfashionable in the modern world that this would be of theoretical interest only. Between pacifism and militarism stands Just War theory which holds that though war is an evil, we can be justified in waging it. The theory as it was developed over some considerable period of time presents us with two sets of principles which must be satisfied if a war is to be just. The first of these consists in the conditions that must be met in going to war – *ad bellum* principles – and those that the conduct of war must meet – *in bello* principles. While there are difficulties with the basis and interpretation of the *ad bellum* principles, appeal to a general framework of natural law makes plausible the idea that resorting to war can be justified, and we further saw that even if the traditional principles are not exactly right, any adequate substitute would have to proceed along broadly similar lines. It is of course idle to show that declaring war can be just, if in fact no war could ever be conducted justly. This is why the *in bello* principles are specially important, and since one of them, the proportionality principle, raises no new issues from its appearance in the first list, it is the principle of the immunity of non-combatants which invites the closest scrutiny. The principle of the immunity of non-combatants faces two major difficulties, the definition of the distinction between combatants and non-combatants and the unavoidability, in nearly all actual wars, of casualties among non-combatants. Examination of the first of these showed that, though the distinction cannot always be easily or clearly drawn, this is not a sufficient ground for thinking that there is no such distinction, and that we can defend the principle by insisting that where it is possible to draw it, as it often is, it should be adhered to. The second problem was not so easily averted. In trying to justify the death and injury to non-combatants which invariably occurs as a side-effect of military action, proponents of Just War theory might appeal to the doctrine of double effect. By making this appeal they are doing no more than moralists have done in other fields, but in deploying the DDE they assume that the most important moral feature of an action is its intention, not its consequences. This is precisely what will be contended by opposing consequentialists, those who hold that the moral worth or wickedness of an action is to be determined entirely by its consequences. The next step in the argument, therefore, is to ask whether they are right, and the use of nuclear weapons provides an important context in which to ask this question.

Nuclear Weapons

There was a brief period in the early Renaissance, it is said, when the armies of the many small states that comprised what we now know as Italy, had perfected strategic positioning to such a degree that, once two armies were in position, it was clear who would win were they to fight, and so no actual fighting ensued. War had become a sort of chess. The historical truth of this rather agreeable picture is questionable, though it has some basis in fact, but two points are clear. First, if such a world ever were the case, the ethics of war, though it would not be entirely redundant, would be much less pressing. Second, the world of modern warfare is not and could not be like this. This is because of the nature of modern weaponry.

By 'modern' here must be meant largely the twentieth century. The invention of machine guns, tanks, long-range missiles and aircraft pushed the destructive power of weaponry far beyond anything previous ages had known. It also greatly increased the indiscrimination of the destruction. Past wars have been very brutal, and very extensive. In the protracted Wars of the Roses (1455–85), for example, it has been estimated that as much as 2 per cent of the entire adult male population of England and Wales was under arms at one time, and, relative to the total population then, the Battle of Towton had an enormous number of casualties. But for all that, death and injury did not extend very far beyond those actually engaged in fighting. The same is true of much more recent times. The horrible injuries and slaughter witnessed in the Crimean War (1854–6), which prompted the innovative work of Florence Nightingale, or of the American Civil War (1860–4), were also largely confined to combatants. (In the early stages of the American Civil War, non-combatants actually turned up, with picnics, to watch the fighting as one would a football match). But the advent of modern weapons altered this beyond measure, and in every major war this century civilian casualties have been high.

Worse was to come, however. At the close of World War II, nuclear weapons were used for the first time, by the Western Allies against Japan. Their power to destroy surpassed anything previous periods could have thought possible. Destruction on this scale cannot discriminate. When people have spoken of 'limited' nuclear war, they have meant war limited in space and time. They did not mean, and could not have meant, war limited to those engaged in fighting it, because with nuclear weapons this is a practical impossibility.

Now those who adhere to the principles of the Just War must encounter a problem with nuclear weapons. At least, in a sense, they encounter one. The problem is not that the theory is difficult to apply. On the contrary, it is easy to apply. In an earlier example we imagined the bombing of a military base close to a hospital. Whatever we say about this, it is clear that the principle requires that weapons which *reduce* the chances of causing innocent casualties must be preferred to those that *increase* it. Since the use of nuclear weapons increases the chances of innocent casualties from a probability to a certainty, a theory of justice in war which requires the distinction between combatant and non-combatant to be observed if at all possible, could never sanction the use of nuclear weapons. It follows that a nuclear war, even one of those known as 'limited', can never be just.

Why should this implication be thought a problem in *any* sense? Here we return to consequentialism. There have been people who have argued, with some plausibility, that the bombing of Hiroshima and Nagasaki at the end of World War II, however ghastly, actually reduced the total number of deaths that might have been expected. To make a calculation of this sort is not easy, and it can never be made with much certainty because it relies on speculative hypotheses about how things would have gone if they had taken a different course, how history *might have been*, rather than how it *was*. Nevertheless, we are often required to make calculations of this sort in everyday life, and there is nothing intrinsically absurd about doing so.

There is no need for present purposes to go into the details of this particular calculation, however. Suffice it to say that, though Germany was defeated (Hitler died in April, Hiroshima was bombed in August, 1945) the state of the war in the Far East was such as to give grounds for the belief that fighting, and with it much death and destruction, could have continued there for some considerable time. This was, after all, the calculation that the Western leaders made. Let us suppose it is correct. From a consequentialist point of view, then, had the Allies not dropped nuclear bombs, they would have been the cause of many more deaths. If so, not only were they *justified* in using the atom bomb, they were *obliged* to do so. Otherwise, they would have knowingly allowed deaths that they could have prevented. Whether consequentialist calculations do support this conclusion in this case is not our main concern. The point is rather that *if* they did, we would have an argument which appears to justify the use of nuclear weapons, and from this possibility we can generalize. That is to say, from the consequentialist point of view, whenever the use of nuclear weapons can be seen to have better consequences than the refusal to use them, they ought to be used.

If we had only our moral intuitions to rely on in this matter, we would have reached a stand-off between consequentialism and Just War theory at this point. Those who regard the use of nuclear weapons with horror will be inclined to commend the Just War theory for failing to accommodate their use. Those who are more impressed by life and death headcounts, will prefer the consequentialist approach, and so reject Just War theory. To proceed further, therefore, we have to look at the theoretical underpinnings and not just at the moral implications. Having examined the basis of Just War theory in some detail already, it is appropriate to examine consequentialism more closely. It should be said, however, that consequentialism is a large and complex topic which moral philosophers have discussed at great length and with a great deal of sophistication. So it will only be possible to touch upon some aspects of it here.

Consequentialism

It is better to prefer fewer deaths to more. So the consequentialist believes, and so most people will think when the principle is abstractly stated in this way. It is less clear that the principle always holds when we attach numbers to it. Is it so very obvious that we should prefer, for example, two million deaths to two million and one? Again, in the abstract, this is perhaps something most people would subscribe to. But if the choice is between actually killing two million people in order to prevent the deaths of two million and one, we may be more inclined to draw back because, whatever the calculations, actually carrying out the slaughter of two million people, albeit for the sake of a net gain of one life, seems too awful to contemplate. Even in the case of much smaller numbers – killing nine to save ten, say – a measure of uncertainty will arise in most minds, because deliberate killing on even this relatively limited scale is something we are deeply inclined against.

The general structure of such cases is this. We are faced with doing something that would normally be thought of as a terrible wrong – mass killing – in order to secure an outcome that is only slightly better. Some philosophers have thought that when the balance of good over evil is this close, what we face is a true moral dilemma, that is to say, a set of circumstances in which whatever we do will be wrong. But a persistent consequentialist need not take this view. There is this to be said after all. Neither of the situations imagined presents us with a *perfect* dilemma. In each case there is a reason to prefer one outcome over another, namely the life that is saved. However, two further important features are missing from the description. We are being asked to consider every life *on a par*, and we are being invited to ignore the manner in which they are lost or saved. The consequentialist has a point if the circumstance is this; I can save ten people if I approach a sinking ship from one side, nine if I approach it from the other, but I cannot save both sets of people. Surely I should go for the side with ten. So much we might all agree with, but imagine a different case in which nine people are held hostage by ten kidnappers. Our choice, let us suppose, is between killing the kidnappers and saving the hostages, or letting the hostages be killed and allowing the kidnappers to live. What a simple calculation based on numbers of lives overlooks is an important difference between these two examples, namely the moral status of the people whose lives they are. The hostages are innocent, and if anyone has to die, it seems that the kidnappers are the ones who deserve to do so. The idea of desert invoked here alters the moral dimensions of the case.

Introducing the second missing feature alters the moral dimension as well. In the boat example, whichever group dies, a tragedy has happened, but no evil act has been performed. I have saved some and failed to save others, but I have not *drowned* anyone. In the second case, if I allow the kidnappers to kill the hostages, I have permitted an evil act to be done. A pacifist would claim, of course, that if I kill the ten hostages this is also the commission of an evil act. But this serves to confirm, not to refute, the claim that the two cases are different from a moral point of view.

It seems then that the moral dimension of a circumstance cannot be explained wholly in terms of simple consequentialist calculations of costs and benefits in terms of lives or welfare. There is also moral status and the nature of action to be considered. These are not unproblematic ideas, however, and something more needs to be said in their defence before they can be said to be real obstacles to consequentialism. Take the nature of action, for instance. Common moral thinking draws a distinction between commission and omission and believes, for example, that it is worse to take a life than to fail to save it, that it is worse to injure someone than to fail to treat their injuries. This is a distinction consequentialists generally dispute, claiming either that ultimately there is no such distinction or that if there is it is of no moral relevance since the bad outcome is the same. Certainly it is not easy to defend this distinction in every context. Take the case of a wealthy relative whose life depends on receiving periodic but regular supplies of oxygen. I might, in order to inherit, kill him by turning off the machine, or by failing to turn it on when he needs it. The first is an act of commission, the second an act of omission, but this does not seem to make much difference to the moral assessment of my action.

The topic is more complex, in fact, than this simple example suggests, but we need not go into all its ramifications here. Let us reserve judgement on the issue of intention and consequence, and for present purposes focus on the idea of moral status. 'She started it' is an appeal that small children very easily and readily learn to make. The fact that they do so indicates a primitive grasp on the important concept of *fault*, which is different to that of *harm*. We can agree with the consequentialist that when harm results from something I do, the following is true:

1 I am the cause of harm.
2 Causing harm is a *prima facie* wrong, that is, something which always calls for justification.

Now consequentialism holds that the form this justification must take is showing that still greater harm has been averted thereby. This is precisely how the consequentialist justification of the bombing of Hiroshima and Nagasaki goes – more lives were saved than would have been lost. But to restrict justification in this way is to *assume* that consequentialism is correct. If we take into account the variety of justifying reasons that people actually give in justification, we can see that there are dimensions which consequentialism ignores. One of these is moral status. It is not just the degree of suffering that matters, but the fault or innocence of those who suffer it.

Moral status in this sense matters a great deal to distinctions that are fundamental to our thinking – crime and punishment for instance. What is the difference between a fine and a theft? The point of fining someone is to inflict a measure of harm, and the harm inflicted – being $50 poorer, say – is exactly the same as that which results from a theft of $50. The difference which justifies the one over the other, then, cannot be a matter of harm inflicted, but the deserts and entitlements of the people involved. The thief is not *entitled* to the $50 which is why he *deserves* to be fined. And this is true irrespective of harm and benefit – the thief might well feel the loss of $50 more than the person who is robbed.

To make this point is not to provide a conclusive refutation of consequentialism, in whose defence further moves can be made; there are consequentialist justifications of punishment, for example. So it should be emphasized once again that the arguments between consequentialism and its critics are complex, and readers who are specially interested are advised to follow up the relevant suggestions for further reading. What the argument can be said to have shown is that the burden of proof falls on the consequentialist to show that it is only the consequences of an action that matter morally, because non-consequentialism is more in keeping with the wider, richer set of concepts common moral thinking employs. Without further persuasive argument on behalf of consequentialism, enough has been said to make plausible the conclusion that any adequate moral theory will have to be non-consequentialist in the sense of lending considerable moral importance to intention and status.

This is precisely what the Just War theory does. Consequentialism rejects some of the principles and resulting reasoning of Just War theory on the grounds that it is outcomes that matter. We have found no reason to support this restriction, however, which is in any case seriously at odds with common forms of moral analysis. This disagreement between consequentialists and Just War theory is in fact evident from the outset, because the very existence of *in bello* as well as *ad bellum* principles implies that in Just War theory the end, however praiseworthy, does not always justify the means, which is what consequentialism implies. From the point of view of justice *in bello*, we can agree that the dropping of the atom bomb saved lives, that saving lives is a just cause, and yet still deny that dropping the bomb was justified. This is because the lives saved (the lives of combatants) do not enjoy the same moral status as those lost (the lives of non-combatants). The former are legitimate targets in war, the latter not. Drawing this distinction allows us to defend the more general claim about nuclear weapons, that their indiscriminate character prevents them from *ever* being used justly. In the present context, this amounts to the conclusion that a *nuclear* war cannot be a *just* war.

Nuclear Deterrence

Nuclear weapons have only been used in war once. Their role in international relations, however, has been far greater than this suggests, because they have played a large part in peacetime, namely as a central element in policies of deterrence. Contemporary nuclear weapons have far more destructive power than those that were used against Japan. They are truly weapons of mass destruction which can destroy vast numbers of people and contaminate huge areas of territory in a very short time. This fact, combined with their importance in relations between the USA and USSR at the height of the Cold War, occasioned extensive and sophisticated debate, amongst moral philosophers, theologians and others, about the ethics of deploying them as a deterrent. With the dramatic change which followed the collapse of the USSR and the Warsaw Pact in the 1980s, attention has tended to shift to other questions. But nuclear weapons continue to be held and sought after for deterrent purposes. This is because there is widespread agreement that their deployment in Europe was beneficial; it did prevent war. Those who have doubts about the morality of deterrence sometimes question this, but it is in so far as nuclear deterrence is thought of as a *successful* policy that it raises interesting and important ethical issues.

If the Just War conclusion that nuclear weapons could never be *used* justly is correct, how could it be morally defensible to *threaten* to use them? This is a natural question to ask, but the answer it implies — that it is not morally defensible — follows only if we assume the following general moral principle: *It is always wrong to threaten to do what it would be wrong to do.* Is this a valid moral principle?

We can show that this principle is not *necessarily* true by invoking consequentialism once more. Consequentialism holds that the wrongness of an action depends upon its consequences. Now, it is obvious that the consequences of threatening to do something, and the consequences of actually doing it, could be quite different. From this it follows that the wrongness of a threat, and the wrongness of performing the action threatened, can also be different. By way of illustration, consider a simple domestic example. I might threaten to send a child to bed for bad behaviour, with the beneficial consequence that her behaviour improves. But if the threat fails, it could be that the tantrum I know would ensue from actually sending her, would count against carrying out the threat.

We have, of course, found against consequentialism in the last section. The only point of referring to it once more is to show that the principle 'It is always wrong to threaten to do what it would be wrong to do' does not hold for every possible moral position. The more precise question we need to ask therefore, is whether it holds for Just War theory.

To explore this issue properly it is necessary to recap a little. Just War theory, unlike consequentialism, is not concerned with actions and outcomes alone. In order to resort to war justly, the aims of the war must themselves be just. Now the aim I have in going to war, is not the *actual* outcome, obviously, since nothing has yet happened, but the *intended* outcome. Thus the justice of the war rests in part on the justice of the intention. The appeal to intention is important, because it suggests an argument which *would* show that, if the actual use of nuclear weapons is unjustifiable, so too is their use as a deterrent.

The argument goes like this:

1 It is morally wrong to intend to do what it would be morally wrong to do.
2 In threatening to do something, I intend to do it, should the threat fail.
3 Therefore, it is wrong to threaten to do what it would be wrong to do.
4 If it is always morally wrong to use nuclear weapons, it is morally wrong to intend to use them.
5 In threatening to use nuclear weapons, I intend to use them.
6 Therefore, it is morally wrong to threaten to use them.
7 Nuclear deterrence relies upon the threat to use nuclear weapons.
8 Therefore nuclear deterrence, no less than nuclear war, is morally wrong.

The conclusion of this argument is sometimes expressed by saying that while the use of nuclear weapons, because of their indiscriminate character, makes those who use them murderers, adopting the strategy of nuclear deterrence requires those who employ it to 'have murder in their hearts'.

Threats, Bluffs and Conditional Intentions

One response to this argument would be to question step 7 — nuclear deterrence relies upon the threat to use nuclear weapons. The word 'threaten' is somewhat ambiguous. It can mean the uttering of threatening words, or it can mean the action of threatening itself. The second sense implies an intention to do what is threatened. The first need not, and when it does not we mark the difference by calling it a 'bluff'. A threat and a bluff may be expressed in the same words. The difference is that the former carries a serious intention, the latter does not. Now why shouldn't a *bluff* be sufficient for deterrent effect? When I issue what seems like a threat, I may be bluffing, but so long as the object of the bluff does not know this, it may be as effective as a genuine threat.

This is a very attractive way out of the problem. It seems to secure the undoubtedly good effects of nuclear deterrence without requiring anyone to have murder in their hearts. But does it? In order for a bluff to be convincing, appearances must be sufficiently deceptive. When we turn from more simple cases to that of nuclear weapons, we are considering circumstances in which a large number of people are involved. These people are related in a chain of command, and the chain of command is only effective if orders issued at one point actually produce actions at another. Now, one thing this means is that there must be a serious intention on the part of those given orders to follow them. Without such an intention, the presidents and prime ministers responsible for policy cannot be said to be deciding matters at all, but merely adding their voices to the general flow of deliberation. It is only if one voice (or set of voices), that of head of state or of government, is decisive, that they can be said to be in control. What this means, however, is that though heads of state might indulge in the moral escape route of bluff, they can do so only if those below them are *not* bluffing, but seriously intend to launch nuclear weapons if ordered to. Does it not follow that, while heads of state might escape moral censure, they do so only at the expense of everyone else in the chain of command, who must indeed 'have murder in their hearts'?

For example, the President of the United States might announce that he will order the use of nuclear weapons, if an opposing power bloc makes aggressive or imperialistic moves in some hitherto neutral part of the world. The opposing power bloc cannot know whether this is bluff or genuine threat, but so long as it *could be* a genuine threat, it will have deterrent force. For the President to maintain this deterrent force, however, supposing he is bluffing, it has to be true (a) that his forces are genuinely ready to carry out his instructions and (b) his own forces, no less than the enemy's are kept in the dark about his true intentions. Thus the military commanders responsible for the silos in which the missiles are kept must fully intend, and be ready to launch weapons of mass destruction against civilian populations, and they must be misled into falsely believing that the President's bluff is a serious threat.

The second of these points is sometimes dismissed on the grounds that those who cavil about white lies when it comes to the use of nuclear deterrence to prevent war, have lost a sense of proportion. But this is too easy. What a successful policy of deterrence which deliberately rested upon a bluff would require, is systematic deception within both the military command and the political system. This is not something to be taken lightly. But the more important point from a philosophical point of view, is that the appeal to bluff escapes the charge of evil intentions only at one level; at every other level, evil intentions remain. It is important to understand this charge clearly. The opponent of nuclear deterrence is not saying that the *cause* in view is evil, but that, albeit in a good cause, those responsible for maintaining an effective nuclear deterrent must fully intend to bring about the deaths of large numbers of innocent non-combatants *if required to do so*, and that to intend this, is to intend to do that which cannot be justified.

It seems then that 'bluff instead of threaten' is not a strategy that will provide the believer in Just War theory with an escape from the conclusion that nuclear deterrence is immoral.

Some philosophers have explored an alternative response to the argument set out above by questioning step 2, and with it step 5 which is its application to the particular case. Is it true that if I threaten to do something under certain conditions, I *must* intend to do it, *should the threat fail*? Am I rationally obliged to follow up the threat? What those who ask this question have in mind is this. In one circumstance, I can issue a threat, and fully intend it. But this is a *conditional* threat in the sense that the rationality of making it depends upon the conditions prevailing at the time it is made. Should the threat fail, I find myself in different circumstances, and we cannot say that in these changed circumstances, my intention must remain unchanged. It was rational to make the threat then, but it is not necessarily rational to carry out the threat. Perhaps it would be best to adopt a different strategy. If I am acting rationally the fact that I have threatened is one consideration when the threat fails to deter, but it is not the only consideration. If this is correct, it cannot be predicted that the intention embodied in the threat, will also be the intention in these altered circumstances. This, it is argued, breaks the connection between the moral position of someone actually performing the action and that of someone merely threatening to do so.

But would a 'conditional' threat serve to deter, if it is not certain that it would be carried out? The answer, it is argued, is 'yes', because uncertainty is enough for deterrence. Though the principles of rational action do not give us reason to predict that the threat will be carried out, they do not give us reason to suppose that it will not, and those who are being threatened, still have reason to be deterred therefore. It might be thought that the problem of requiring serious intention on the part of those lower down the chain of command, which defeated the attempt to make do with bluff, undermines this response also. But if heads of state can avail themselves of the middle ground of the 'conditional threat', which does not require them to have murder in their hearts, so too can all those in the chain of command.

Is this then the solution to the Just War theorists' problem? We can threaten to use weapons of mass destruction, seriously but conditionally intend to do so, and, nevertheless, leave open the question whether we ever determine to destroy people. It has to be said that not everyone has been convinced by the concept of a conditional threat, and there is a measure of obscurity about this line of thought which is not altogether satisfactory. The best that can be said, perhaps, is that this is an idea worth exploring closely, if there is no other solution available.

But there is at least one other possibility. This arises from the possibility of what are sometimes called 'nested' intentions. Different intentions need not be exclusive. For example, I can intend to catch the train at four, and I can intend to visit my aunt in hospital. Not only are these not mutually exclusive, but the former can be part of the latter. I can intend to catch the train as part of my intention to visit my aunt. Now, when it is said that it is wrong to intend to do what it would be wrong to do, it is assumed that 'to do' describes the same action. There may be nothing incorrect in this assumption, but it is inclined to mislead us when we are thinking about deterrence, because the intention I have when I threaten someone, may be nested in a quite different intention from that which I would have were I to carry out my threat. If so, it is possible that the higher intention when I threaten is different to that were I to carry out the threat, and of a different moral order.

To see this we have to think about the intention within which the threat posed by nuclear deterrence is nested. When I threaten to use nuclear weapons, it is true that I intend to use them. But this is not the proper overall description of my intention. How could it be? My purpose is precisely *not* to have to use the weapons; my intention is to preserve peace, and this is a morally laudable intention. Should deterrence fail, and I use the weapons, my intention in using them could no longer be to preserve peace but, for instance, to retaliate or exact revenge. Retaliation, at the cost of thousands of innocent lives, let us agree with the Just War theorist, would be morally deplorable. But now we have a morally significant difference between the threat and the use of nuclear weapons. To threaten to use them as part of a policy of deterrence has the intention of *protecting* innocent lives; their use has the intention of *taking* them. It is only if we fail to take into account the higher level intentions within which the intention to use nuclear weapons is nested (preserving peace versus exacting revenge), that we could think of the role of nuclear weapons in deterrence as no less culpable than their use in war.

Mutually Assured Destruction

The ethics of nuclear deterrence, it should now be clear, is a complex subject, and the solution of 'nested intentions' seems the most promising line of defence for the idea that nuclear deterrence can be morally acceptable. Of course it is not enough that such a policy be morally defensible, but that it also be effective, and we might ask therefore whether it has deterrent force. If it is known that the actual use of nuclear weapons is regarded as absolutely forbidden, how can their possession as a deterrent ever be convincing? The answer lies in the strategy known as 'mutually assured destruction'.

At the height of the Cold War, defence strategists favoured a policy of mutually assured destruction. This was commonly referred to by its acronym MAD, and to many it appeared just that. How could it be other than the utmost madness to defend oneself in such a way that, should the defence fail, the destruction of virtually the whole world would ensue? It was this thought which led to alternative strategies of more limited nuclear response.

Mutually assured destruction is a policy by which one side's use of nuclear weapons automatically triggers a conflict which no one can win. Everyone loses because everyone is destroyed. The thinking behind this invoked principles of rational self-interest rather than ethical propriety. That is to say, it was believed that if the price of using nuclear weapons was known to be total annihilation, it could never be in anyone's interest to use them, and so however much the power blocs armed themselves, there was a guarantee that they would never be used.

Defence strategists have argued at length about the conception of mutually assured destruction. Here, however, our interest is in the ethical dimension of the policy. Could it ever be morally right to run the risk of destroying the whole world? Interestingly, there is good reason to think that the answer is 'yes'.

To appreciate this possibility it is first necessary to observe that we live in a world where nuclear weapons exist and cannot, as has often be said, be uninvented. There is thus *always* a risk that they will be used. Moreover, *any* use of the sort of nuclear weapons that now exist would result in massive loss of human and animal lives, and the destruction of culture and environment. The bombing of Japan is not a test case. These were relatively small bombs used by one side with no possibility of retaliation by the other. It was not a nuclear *conflict*. But in a true conflict, with modern weapons, the devastation would be enormous.

Given then that there is in *every* strategy *some* risk, the rational assessment of risk must take the form of multiplying the cost of outcome by the probability of its happening – it is rational to prefer to run a very great danger which there is little likelihood of happening, to a much lesser danger which is very likely to happen. Thus, though the cost of mutual destruction is gigantic, if the strategy drastically reduces the probability of nuclear conflict to almost zero, it may be the less risky policy to pursue. Sometimes this has been doubted. People have argued that the cost of total annihilation is infinite and that infinity multiplied by however small a probability is still infinity. But this is not correct. It is true that were the world to be destroyed, every good thing would cease to be. But so would every *evil* thing. There is an alternative scenario to total annihilation. It is one in which just some people and animals continue to live, but they do so through centuries of untold suffering. Arguably this is a *worse* outcome than the destruction of everything. It follows that the cost of total annihilation cannot be infinite because we can imagine something even worse.

What this line of reasoning appears to show then is that the policy of mutually assured destruction may be the best one to adopt, if what we are concerned with is the minimization of risk to human life and civilization. However, this does not reach the heart of the ethical question with which we are concerned, which relates to the injustice of the use of nuclear weapons and the relation of this to nuclear deterrence. The deployment of nuclear weapons as part of an intention to preserve peace and protect people from destruction, we have seen, is morally justifiable. What is not morally justifiable is the decision to use those weapons once the deterrent has failed. Now an automatic system of mutually assured destruction is relevant here because it eliminates the need for decision, and hence the moral relevance of decision. The position is like one in which I set up a system of automatic payment. As work is done, it is paid for by the system; it does not need a decision on my part. Similarly, MAD is a system in which *anyone*'s use of nuclear weapons automatically triggers mutual destruction. This is the point of the strategy. Consequently, there is no question of anyone's *deciding* to use them. It simply happens. Relying on a system of automatic response may or may not be morally justifiable. This is a quite general question with which we are not directly concerned here. The relevant point is that by precluding the possibility of taking *any* decision, it precludes the possibility of taking a morally wrong decision. The strategy of MAD is such that, the enemy can know that I will never use nuclear weapons (because I believe it is immoral to do so), and yet *also* know that his first use of them will result in his destruction. It is in this way justice and deterrence are *both* secured by a policy of mutually assured destruction.

Many people who read arguments in which the idea of mutually assured destruction is given serious attention often have a strong sense of entering the lunatic world of *Dr Strangelove* (Stanley Kubrick's black comedy of the Cold War, with Peter Sellers in the title role). In a world of nuclear weapons, however, whose horrifying character can scarcely be comprehended, it is not surprising if we have to entertain thoughts, and accept conclusions, deeply at odds with what we have been accustomed to think before. The more surprising thing is that human beings should ever have thought of inventing nuclear weapons at all.

Ironically, their invention may have undermined the reason for their being invented, and eliminated the very advantages the argument we have been considering suggests. The strategy of MAD makes the cost of using nuclear weapons too high ever to be contemplated. This, let us suppose, renders nuclear war extremely unlikely, a very desirable outcome. But by the same token, it means that their deterrent effect with respect to ordinary *non-nuclear* war is seriously reduced. If the powers that possess these weapons are unlikely ever to use them, those who would wage war on a conventional level, have no reason to fear escalation to the nuclear level. Conventional war, as this century amply demonstrates, can be the cause of death, destruction, dislocation and suffering on a gigantic scale. Those who invented the nuclear bomb seem to have been motivated in part by the hope that a weapon of such power would put an end to all war. Their purpose, in other words, was not to deter *nuclear* war, but war as such, and many politicians still hold that the existence of nuclear weapons has secured fifty years of peace in Europe. Unfortunately, whatever about the original atom-bomb, the power of the weaponry that came to be developed has generated a logic of deterrence almost completely subversive of this hopeful purpose. Because war using nuclear weapons is highly unlikely, war using every other kind of weapon is more likely.

In short, the world of nuclear weapons, with its awesome possibility of annihilation, is a world which human beings cannot now escape, but which does little to ameliorate the dangers that existed before it was ever created.

Summary

We have spent two chapters on the ethics of war and nuclear weapons not only because the arguments are complex and difficult, but because war, and Cold War, constitute the high (or low) point of international relations. What we have seen is that the traditional theory of the Just War, though it was formulated in a world very different to that in which we live today, and rests upon a conception of natural law which has become unfashionable in modern times, retains a great deal of plausibility. The arguments have shown that a war can be just, and that to be so, the resort to war and the conduct of it must satisfy two sets of principles broadly similar to those which the Just War theorists elaborated. In particular, the principles of authoritative declaration, just cause, proportionality and the immunity of non-combatants can all be supported by convincing if not conclusive arguments. To accept such principles, however, carries the clear implication that the use of nuclear weapons in war could never be justified. Many people have thought that from this it follows that a policy of nuclear deterrence cannot be justified either, but after examining several interconnected lines of thought, we have found good reason in favour of the moral defensibility of such a policy.

War, as we have been considering it, is the recourse to arms between states. Not all wars are of this kind; some are civil, that is, within one state. Nor is all recourse to arms necessarily war. One state might invade another, as the US did Grenada, to force an outcome it thinks desirable without provoking a war between the two states. Can this ever be justified? This is the topic of the next chapter.

Suggestions for further reading

Henry Shue (ed.), *Nuclear Deterrence and Moral Restraint.*
Douglas Lackey, *Moral Principles and Nuclear Weapons.*
Paul Ramsay, 'The Limits of Nuclear War'.
Peter Singer (ed.), *A Companion to Ethics,* relevant entries: Jeff McMahan, 'War and Peace'; Philip Pettit, 'Consequentialism'.
Michael Walzer, *Just and Unjust Wars,* chs 16 and 17.

5

Intervention

Armed invasion of one country by another was a very familiar part of the world of empires. It was also the cause of the two greatest wars ever known. World War I properly began when Germany under Kaiser Wilhelm invaded Belgium, and World War II when Germany, this time under Adolf Hitler, invaded Czechoslovakia. Both invasions were regarded as acts of aggression. If this is the correct description, and there is little reason to doubt it, they were of course indefensible in the light of Just War principles. From the point of view of justice and injustice the circumstances of World War I are more complicated than World War II, but in both cases there is a plausible case to be made that Germany, however legitimate its grievances, by the very fact of invading the territory of another state, violated the principles of international justice. Consequently, the countries which had recourse to arms in response could rightly claim that they were acting in a just cause. Armed invasion seems the unmistakable mark of the aggressor, and resistance to it automatically a just cause.

But is this correct? Could it ever be *just* to initiate an armed invasion?

International Law

If we were to treat this as a question of international law, there is no doubt about the answer: it is unlawful to invade another country on any ground whatever. This principle is enshrined in almost every international agreement made since World War II. For instance, the *Charter of the Organization of American States* of 1948, in Article 15, affirms quite categorically: *No state or group of states has the right to intervene directly or indirectly, for any reason whatever, in the internal or external affairs of any other State.* A similar sort of principle will be found in the *Charter of the Organization of African Unity*, and in agreements linking countries in the Far East. But the most emphatic, most comprehensive, and universally applicable pronouncement of this kind is found in the United Nations *Declaration on Principles of International Law*. Expanding on the principle 'concerning the duty not to intervene in matters within the domestic jurisdiction of any State' it says:

> No state or group of States has the right to intervene directly or indirectly for any reason whatever, in the internal or external affairs of any other state.
>
> Consequently, armed intervention and all other forms of interference or attempted threats against the personality of the State or against its political, economic and cultural elements are in violation of international law. No State may use or encourage the use of economic, political or any other type of measures to coerce another State in order to obtain from it advantages of any kind. Also no State shall organize, assist, foment, incite, or tolerate subversive terrorist or armed activities directed towards the violent overthrow of or civil strife in another State. (Brownlie, 1995, p. 40)

International law, then, is clear. It proscribes any form of intervention for whatever reason. The term 'international law' here refers to the positive content of specific agreements between states, and to the principles that are widely accepted in the conduct of relations between states by legal bodies such as the

International Court of Justice. In earlier chapters we have seen reason to distinguish between such 'positive' law on the one hand and 'natural' law on the other. We have also seen reason to think that the idea of natural law applies to relations between states as well as within them. *Natural* law, if we follow the conclusions of previous chapters, is not concerned to expound what positive law *is*, but what it *ought* to be. So, however clear positive international law is in what it says on the topic of intervention, there is still a moral philosophical question to raise — what ought it to say?

This is an interesting and important question with respect to any branch of law. In the case of international law, however, it has additional significance. As has been noted several times already, the international arena differs from the national in lacking a single, sovereign power, charged with enforcement, and this is a matter of some practical consequence. Though there *are* international legal institutions (the International Court of Justice being the most obvious), countries quite often refuse to come to the bar of them. This is true not just of what we might think of as 'rogue' members of the global community, but major members such as the USA, which in the 1980s refused to appear to answer charges about its conduct towards Nicaragua. When this happens, the institutions in question have no effective powers of enforcement. They cannot compel the representatives of a country to appear, and they cannot ensure that any penalty they may determine will be imposed. Sometimes countries refuse to accept the authority of the Court because they dispute the moral legitimacy of the principles upon which a case against them is being brought, so that unlike a domestic case within one country, the authority of international institutions of law rests directly on questions of moral right. This lends further importance and significance to the question of the moral basis of international law.

And so the question arises: ought there to be an absolute ban on intervention in the affairs of one country by another? This is not now a question for lawyers to grapple with, but one for moral philosophy.

Autonomy and the Nation State

It was noted in the first chapter that the doctrine of national self-
determination has come to play a very large part in modern
thinking about international relations. It is a doctrine closely
connected with the ethical proscription on intervention. If a
nation should determine its own affairs, which is what self-
determination means, it should have its own state. This was the
idea that so influenced the settlement of Europe after World War
I and which shaped the character of post-colonial Africa and Asia.
Once, under the inspiration of this idea, the nation state is
created, its inviolability seems a natural inference to draw. If each
nation ought to have its own state, and if by being given
statehood each nation is given charge over its own affairs, it
surely follows that national self-determination should be protected. If so, the principles of international law, described in
the last section, which outlaw intervention absolutely, can be
seen to derive legitimacy from the doctrine of national self-
determination.

On first appearances, at any rate, this reasoning seems clear,
and can be made even more plausible by considering the parallel
between national self-determination and self-determination on
the part of individuals. When human beings are very young
children, their affairs – what they eat, when they sleep, the
clothes they wear and so on – are determined almost entirely by
their parents or guardians. This is because they are not capable of
determining these things in their own best interests for themselves. The process of growing up can best be thought of as an
education away from dependency on the will of *others* to the
exercise of one's *own* will. To have become an adult is not just
to have attained physical and psychological maturity, but to have
secured the right to decide such things for oneself.

It is important to note that there is a difference between self-
determination, more commonly known as 'autonomy' and welfare. Though the possession of autonomy is no doubt a good
thing for most people in the sense that it enhances their general
welfare, its being good for them is not what makes it their right.

The right of self-determination is based on the fact that adults are free and equal and the exercise of the freedom that comes from equality can be to the detriment of the individual. As a child I can be prevented from smoking cigarettes by my parents on the grounds that it is not good for me; as an adult, it is no better for me, but whether I smoke or not is for me, not anyone else to decide. The decision, for good *or* ill, is mine by right. It is not that having reached adulthood, I am certain to take the best decisions on my own behalf. We know that people can make decisions that are highly detrimental to their own interests. The point is, rather, that whether I take good decisions or bad, no one else has the right to take them for me. Adults are vastly superior to newborn children in knowledge, competence and experience. Education, in the broadest sense, steadily reduces this gap, and the point at which the child attains adulthood is that at which all are broadly equal. It is at this point that they become autonomous, having the same right of self-determination as everyone else.

This concept of autonomy is of great moral significance. Respecting other people in their own person (usually known more simply as 'respect for persons') is more fundamental, morally speaking, than attending to their welfare, important though that is. We can see this at the other end of life. Those who fall into senile dementia may be very well cared for, and they may be happy enough in their dotage. But this is small consolation, because their *fundamental* loss is neither welfare nor happiness, which they may retain, but the freedom of ordering their lives for themselves. They have lost their autonomy. Respect for persons is respecting the autonomy of all those capable of exercising it.

The moral concept of autonomy, which is invoked here in establishing the rights of individuals, has played a very important part in relations between states also. Indeed on some occasions the discussion of the right to political autonomy has closely followed the same lines. In debates about the end of empire and the release of Asian and African states from colonial status, for example, part of the dispute was about whether colonial peoples were or were not *capable* of controlling their own affairs. Those who favoured the continuation of empire tended to describe such 'emerging' nations as though they were still in some sort of childhood, and those who argued for their political autonomy argued on the basis of equality. While the first group claimed, with some reason, that *national* government might not lead to *good* government, the opposing group claimed that, good or not, it was theirs by *right*.

The Right of Non-intervention

On the strength of this analysis it seems correct to say that, just as adult human beings have a right to determine their affairs for themselves, so nations have a right to determine *their* affairs for themselves. And just as the right to personal autonomy requires others to stand by when individuals make choices that prove detrimental to their welfare, so the right to national autonomy requires other states to stand by and allow each indigenous nation to sort out its own affairs. To attribute autonomy or the right of self-determination to each state, therefore, is, so to speak, to throw a protective moral barrier against intervention around it, and thus to establish a right of non-intervention.

If this analysis is correct, we have found a moral basis for the absolute ban on intervention enshrined in international law. The law, we might say, grants to each state *legal* protection against intervention, because each state has a *moral* right to political autonomy. In this way we can provide a justification of international law even in the absence of enforcement – international law deserves the respect of those subject to it, not because they can be forced to obey it, but because it embodies the moral rights of nations.

But *is* this analysis of the moral dimensions of intervention and non-intervention correct? In chapter 2 we examined at some length the use of the analogy between the domestic and the international. It is clear that elements of this analogy are at work in this explanation of the moral basis of political autonomy. To speak of 'emergent' nations as 'young', or of ethnic groups as not yet 'mature' enough for self-government, is clearly to suppose that the history of a nation is something like the history of an individual – that is to say, that it can be described as a movement from infancy to adolescence to maturity. Now, nations do have histories, but it should be obvious that talk of their 'childhood' or 'adolescence' can only be figurative. The 'birth' of a nation (a very familiar expression) is a political, not a biological process. Figurative language has its uses, but it can also mislead, and, as we saw earlier, it can mislead if and when it causes us to overlook disanalogies between the moral relations in which individuals stand and the political relations which hold between states.

The analogy between the autonomy of adult human beings and the autonomy of states has to be examined more closely, but if we assume for the moment that it holds, we might still wonder whether drawing it justifies an *absolute* ban on intervention. The UN declaration quoted at the start of this chapter states quite unequivocally that 'no state or group of states has the right to intervene directly or indirectly, *for any reason whatever*'. Would a comparable principle with respect to human beings hold? Are there no grounds upon which we may intervene in the affairs of another?

We are here concerned with intervention for the individual's *own* good. It is plain enough that there can be reason to intervene in the affairs of adults for the safety and protection of *others*. Now there are some circumstances where we can justify interfering in the conduct of another adult human being for their own good. One such circumstance is where we have reason to believe that the individual is not really acting out of free choice. Two familiar examples illustrate this possibility. Many Mental Health Acts give powers to relatives and/or doctors to compel someone to receive treatment for psychological illness even when this is contrary to the express wishes of the patient. Such powers are usually set around with safeguards, because such powers can be used simply to override the autonomy of the patient. But they acknowledge the fact that serious mental illness can undermine a person's rationality and hence their ability to choose freely. A striking instance of this sort of intervention is when a person lost in (curable) depression is prevented from committing suicide.

A second (slightly more contentious) example of morally permissible intervention, concerns membership of cults. It is often
claimed that individuals can be 'brainwashed' by the religious
or political cults with which they have got caught up, and that
the only way to liberate them is to ignore their express wish to
remain with the cult and forcibly remove them. This is more
contentious because it is less clear that there is indeed such a
thing as 'brainwashing' than it is that people suffer from mental
illness.

There are other contexts in which we would agree that it is
morally justifiable to intervene in the actions of an otherwise
autonomous adult, but these two are sufficient. First, they show
that autonomy, though it does constitute a moral barrier around
individuals, is not to be regarded as absolute. In the language of
the law, it is defeasible. That is to say, though normally the
individual's autonomy is sacrosanct, in some circumstances it is
possible to justify disregarding it. Certainly, the onus is always on
those who intervene to show that they are justified in doing so,
but some such justifications are possible. Second, the examples
we have considered suggest one general ground upon which
moral justification can be based, namely the absence of a real
power of choice. The decisions and actions of an individual have
to be the outcome of the right sort of process, namely free
(though not necessarily wise) deliberation, before their autonomy
commands absolute respect.

It is not hard to see the political parallel. The actions of a state
have to be the outcome of the right sort of process before they
can be accorded immunity from intervention. Just what this
process is in the political case is a complex question. To require
a wholly democratic process, for example, would render the
decisions of most states liable to intervention since the number of
properly democratic countries, even on a fairly wide conception
of democracy, is small. But we can content ourselves with less
than this. Let us accept that any political process widely regarded
as legitimate by the citizens of a country, whether or not it can
be described as democratic, is sufficient to bestow the right of
autonomy on decisions reached through it. Even so, it is easy to
find examples where the normal political processes of a country

are deranged, and their legitimacy thereby called into question. In such circumstances it would seem, if we are following the domestic analogy, intervention from outside the country is justifiable. How then could a ban as absolute ('for any reason whatever') as that enshrined in the UN declaration be warranted?

The case against an absolute ban is strengthened when we consider one specific kind of intervention which has exercised theorists of international relations. This is action called 'humanitarian intervention'. There are distressingly many instances in recent history where corrupt and incompetent governments have allowed (sometimes even encouraged) criminality or famine to flourish among their own citizens. It is important to stress that in many of these cases the governments in question retain international recognition and face no serious civil unrest or political rivalry at home, so that their being the holders of state power is not in question. Where widespread suffering caused or exacerbated by the policies of the state is evident, and where another state or group of states has the ability to intervene effectively, what reason could there be for failing to intervene? Nearly all theories of the state – liberal, democratic, socialist and traditionalist – hold that the responsibility of the state, any state, is to protect people from the erosion of liberty, victimization by criminals, and economic devastation. If so, why should this responsibility stop exclusively at the borders of one country, as the UN declaration implies that it should. Is this not an instance of what philosophers have sometimes termed 'rule worship', and precisely the sort of indefensible adherence to national sovereignty which the internationalism discussed in chapter 1 called into question? The doctrine of national sovereignty forbids intervention in the affairs of another state, but the case of humanitarian intervention calls that doctrine into question.

States as Persons

It should be remembered that this doubt about the absolute right of non-intervention has arisen even though we have been assuming that the parallel between nation states and individual human beings holds good. If we call it into question, the case for non-intervention appears to be even worse.

The UN declaration, in its proscription of intervention, contains a somewhat curious phrase – 'armed intervention and all other forms of interference or attempted threats against *the personality of the State*'. What does this mean exactly? The idea that states are corporate *persons* is to be found in the writings of a number of political theorists, notably G. W. F. Hegel (1770–1831). Now, whatever sense we can attach to this idea, it is not hard to show that the disanalogies between states and persons identified in chapter 2 are significant in the discussion of non-intervention. Most important of these is the fact that an individual person constitutes a moral unity in a way that the state does not. This means, among other things, that while it is not possible for there to be a violation of rights in the self-regarding actions of a person, it is possible for there to be a violation of rights within the self-regarding actions of a state.

To see this, consider again the idea of personal autonomy. A person capable of free deliberation may deliberate badly. For example, I can squander my resources to my own detriment. To respect my autonomy, others do not have to regard my decisions as wise. They can recognize only too well that I am acting in ways that are harmful to me. But doubting the wisdom of my actions does not in itself call into question my autonomy. To respect my autonomy other people are not required to approve of me; they are only required to leave me to my own devices. The case is different if I am squandering *someone else's* money, because, while in both cases harm is being done by resources being wasted, the second involves the rights of others. I am entitled to spend my own money as I wish, however foolishly, but I am not entitled to spend other people's.

Not all cases in which I harm others constitutes a violation of their rights, but some, like this one, do, whereas, when I harm myself there can be no violation of right. I cannot steal from myself, or commit physical assault upon myself. Now people do use reflexive language about states. A state, for instance, is sometimes described as tearing itself apart. But this is figurative language. The reality it refers to is one in which groups of people are killing and injuring each other. In such instances there is always extensive violation of rights, and usually relatively innocent parties bear the brunt of this. Where the violation of rights is perpetrated by the agents of the state (the army, police and so on), as part of government policy perhaps, reflexive language ('a country at war with itself', for instance) is seriously misleading, because it disguises the fact that in these cases there is a moral dimension which is necessarily absent in the case of individual human beings. To stand back in such circumstances is not, as it would be in the case of an individual, to respect the freedom to determine one's own affairs adversely, but to tolerate the freedom of some people to determine the affairs of other people adversely. In short, even if there is good reason to think of the state as in some sense 'a person', political autonomy is not analogous with personal autonomy.

This seems to destroy the case for absolute non-intervention completely. In the case of personal autonomy there is a morally explicable presumption that autonomy should be respected. Even here that presumption is defeasible; a case can be made out for intervention in special circumstances. But with the political 'autonomy' of states there is not even that presumption, from which it follows that on the strength of the arguments rehearsed so far, we have found no good reason to subscribe to the absolute right of non-intervention embodied in international law.

Consequentialism and Non-intervention

We have seen that the attempt to base an absolute right to non-intervention in international relations on the model of personal autonomy fails. It fails twice over, in fact, because, if we *grant* the analogy we have no reason to think the right absolute, and if we *deny* the analogy we have no reason to think that there is any such right at all.

The argument which has brought us to this conclusion takes the idea of a right as basic. Not all moral theories share this assumption. Perhaps a different *kind* of argument would produce a conclusion more favourable to non-intervention, just the sort of argument, in fact, as is to be found in the consequentialist approach to ethics, some of whose elements we have already considered. And since consequentialist defences of non-intervention have played a significant part in explanatory defences of international law, there is good reason to explore the consequentialist alternative further in this context.

Consequentialism, it will be recalled, holds that the best justification of a course of action is that it is the action calculated to have the best consequences. This way of expressing the consequentialist approach focuses upon the justification of *action*. However, there can be consequentialist defences of *rules* as well as actions. Although we could, in principle, assess the merits of each and every act on the basis of the consequences it is likely to have, in real life this would often be impracticable. Such calculations take time and effort and to have to do this every time we proposed to act, would be seriously incapacitating. The formulation of general rules of conduct gets round this difficulty. They offer us guidance about what to do, without the necessity of exploring each and every case in detail.

Some moral theories, such as those founded on natural law and those founded on basic rights, conceive of general rules of conduct as moral *principles* which ought to govern and constrain conduct *irrespective* of consequences. Thus a rule against murder or theft would be defended by the first on the grounds that murder and theft are contrary to natural law, and by the second that they are violations of fundamental moral rights. By contrast, for a consequentialist, such rules are helpful guides, not fundamental principles, and they are to be defended, just as individual actions or policies are, by an appeal to the consequences of having them or not having them. Consequentialists would argue that the rules which make up law or morality, for instance, rules against theft and murder, are justified because they are conducive to the general welfare. We are better off if we have such rules than if we do not.

Now a consequentialist defence of a rule of non-intervention in international relations is simply an application of this general approach to the justification of rules. A consequentialist would argue that the absolute proscription of intervention makes for a more peaceful and harmonious international order. If international law were to approve even a limited class of international interventions, this would result in more frequent armed conflicts between states, and this in turn would increase the probability of war and all its undesirable aspects.

One problem with this argument is a theoretical one, namely that a consequentialist theory can never justify an absolute rule of conduct, that is, a rule which admits of no exceptions. For example, if it is wise to have a rule against murder, this is, on the consequentialist's account, because it minimizes death and suffering. But there will always be special, and no doubt highly exceptional circumstances, where it would seem that to murder would reduce death and suffering more than to fail to do so. This was the belief of those who conspired to murder Hitler. The general point is this: how could a justification in terms of consequences *ever* prefer that a rule be kept when breaking it would have better consequences?

The consequentialist might reply by saying that choosing a course of action in the light of estimated consequences is always uncertain. We may *think* that the consequences of breaking a rule like the rule against murder would be better, but we can never be sure of this, partly because of the precedent which our breaking it may establish. The safest course, therefore, is always to follow the rule. But this is not a satisfactory response to the difficulty. In order to arrive at a consequentialist justification of the rule in the first place we have to be able to assess the consequences of individual actions. After all, the justification of the rule is simply a generalization from experience of particular cases. It follows that, in principle, we have to be able to assess the consequences of particular actions. Now, it may be true that in nearly every case the consequences of, say, committing murder are worse than any benefits we might have anticipated. But, since this is an empirical matter, it cannot be declared in advance that this will always be the case. From this it follows that a consequentialist justification of the rule of non-intervention cannot show that rule to be absolute. If it can ever be shown with confidence that breaking the rule on this one occasion would make for a better outcome than not doing so, from a consequentialist point of view we are not only permitted, but obliged to break it.

The Definition of Intervention

Neither the appeal to national autonomy, or a more straightforward consequentialist argument can justify an absolute rule of non-intervention. The failure of both these approaches might lead us to ask whether this is something we ought to try to justify anyway. The only reason we have had for doing so is that international law enshrines an absolute ban on one country interfering in the affairs of another, and from the point of view of the ethics of international relations we are always free to conclude that international law cannot be defended in this case.

In support of this conclusion it is worth noting that, as a matter of fact, intervention by one country in the affairs of another is a reasonably common occurrence, despite the provisions of international law. The reality is sometimes disguised by the fact that discussion of intervention often tacitly assumes that what is under discussion is armed intervention, either by the active support of armed groups within the country, or by armed invasion. But of course intervention takes other forms. Human rights abuses in many countries have been the subject of a range of actions from government representations to the severing of diplomatic relations to trade sanctions. South Africa under apartheid was often the object of policies of this sort. Diplomatic isolation and trade sanctions are frequently thought to be legitimized by their being the co-ordinated actions of more than one country, and where they are, references are often made to action by 'the international community'. But despite the air of legitimacy that this label is intended to give, the principles of the United Nations are quite clear in such circumstances. Intervention on the part of a *group* of countries is outlawed no less than that on the part of one country.

Faced with intervention by diplomatic representation or even trade sanctions, the plausibility of trying to establish a moral justification for an absolute ban seems considerably weakened. Confusion over the ethics of intervention arises from a lack of clarity about the subject of discussion. The definition of intervention rests upon purpose, not upon method. An act, whether relatively mild, like representation, or of great seriousness, like armed invasion, counts as intervention if its purpose is the defence or well-being of the subjects of a country other than that which does the intervening. Trade embargoes intended to assist black or coloured South Africans from the effects of apartheid, for example, are examples of intervention, while embargoes of the very same kind which are intended to protect European commercial interests, say, are not.

Diplomatic protestations can be counterproductive, and trade sanctions are generally ineffectual. There are consequentialist calculations to be made about these, and an ethics of consequentialism therefore has something to say about intervention at this level. It is quite unclear, however, that there are any very well grounded general rules available to guide us here; it seems more reasonable to consider each case on its merits. Consequentialism, therefore, has little that is general to say. But an ethics based on rights or autonomy seems to have nothing at all to say. It can hardly be thought that every sovereign state has a right not to receive representations on the part of some of its subjects, or that its autonomy is violated when such representations are made.

What these remarks suggest is that the ethics of intervention should be restricted to intervention of a more serious kind, namely armed intervention, and that the ethics of intervention should seek to circumscribe these in some way. In the discussion of arguments from national autonomy and general consequences, however, this distinction was not made, but the arguments still failed. What this shows is that neither approach will be satisfactory in the attempt to produce an ethics of armed intervention. In the attempt to find a more satisfactory approach, then, there is reason to return to Just War theory, whose express concern is with the use of arms. And it will have succeeded if its application justifies armed intervention in a very restricted class of cases.

Intervention and Just War Theory

Armed intervention can take two forms. The first is the arming (or lending of military support) to some group within another country for the purpose of aiding them in their efforts on behalf of members of that country. The second is armed invasion of one country by another on behalf of (and not necessarily at the request of) some of its subjects. Now, it is important to see that intervention necessarily falls short of another sort of action which might use either of these as methods, namely conquest. Suppose that in a neighbouring country political conditions are so bad that its citizens are wholly unprotected by the law and constantly subject to poverty, crime and gross rights violations by police or army. One attempted means of protecting them might be out-right conquest, to end the political sovereignty of their own country and make them citizens of another. The alternative of intervening, even by force of arms, thus has this distinguishing characteristic: it recognizes the independence of the country where intervention is contemplated and seeks to take steps which will preserve it. This is an important difference, as we shall see, if any such intervention is circumscribed by the principles of the Just War.

It is not hard to see how these principles are to be adapted. They would read as follows:

1   Armed intervention must be undertaken and waged exclusively by the leaders of the state.
2   Armed intervention must be in a just cause.
3   Recourse to armed intervention must be a last resort.
4   There should be a formal declaration of the intention to intervene by means of arms.
5   Those engaging in armed intervention must have a reasonable hope of success.

6 The evil and damage which armed intervention entails must be judged proportionate to the injustice which occasions it.

7 Actions taken in armed intervention must be proportionate to their objective.

8 Non-combatants must be immune from attack.

Some of the same problems arise here as arise with the original version of these principles relating to war. However, we have already discussed the general cogency of Just War theory, and the purpose here is to see how they would relate to and regulate the special case of armed intervention.

One obvious restriction appears immediately. If the first of these amended principles is accepted, requiring as it does that intervention be not only undertaken but waged by the leaders of a state, armed intervention in the form of support for indigenous military groups would be unjustifiable. We saw that there is reason to qualify the first principle of the Just War in any case, to include groups who can claim some measure of authority for their actions. The precise determination of this idea of authority is unclear, however, and we could not conclude therefore that this first principle would set any very substantial restrictions on intervention. Consequently, we must look to the other principles to secure this. The principles of special interest in this connection are 2, 3 and 5.

That armed intervention must be in a just cause (2) is a principle raising difficulties we have already encountered. But granted that there can be just causes for war, the extension of the principle is clear. It can only be just to undertake armed intervention on behalf of the citizens of another country on grounds which would justify the use of arms in defence of the citizens of one's own. Arguably, this removes some of the problems, since we are not here concerned with two competing conceptions of justice. Furthermore, we can introduce a plausible restriction, namely that arms may only ever be used for humanitarian intervention, where for instance there is gross and widespread violation of rights, where civil strife has reached gargantuan proportions, or where destitution and starvation face a large section of the population. These causes would have justified intervention in Cambodia under Pol Pot, in the terrible slaughter in Rwanda and in the Ethiopian famine. Serious intervention did not take place in any of these instances, but for all that these are good test cases for the principle of non-intervention enshrined in international law.

That armed intervention should be a last resort (3) shares the same rationale here as it does in the resort to war. All use of arms is costly in terms of lives and suffering and any alternative which can plausibly be thought effective to the same end is for that reason to be preferred.

Most interesting of the principles is (5) in fact. Recall that intervention falls short of conquest. This means that the intervening power must either immediately or eventually work through third parties, those indigenous groups who are assisted, or the government which is given control when the direct intervention has ended. Now this, since it removes a substantial element of control from the intervener thus reduces the probability of precise intentions being carried out successfully. It does so in large part because the third parties are by the nature of the case independent agents with aims and policies of their own. The position is not that of principal to agent, as in the case of client to lawyer, but of principal to principal, as in business transactions between partners. So for instance, when the USA under President Clinton actively intervened in the politics of Haiti to reinstate President Aristide, it did so in order to end the harsh and undemocratic military regime which had ousted him. Leaving aside any other interests the USA may have had, the aim was to restore democracy and improve the lot of Haitian citizens. But the accomplishment of this aim depended crucially on the intention and effectiveness of Aristide once returned to power, not as a puppet, but as an independent agent, and whatever the facts of this particular case, it is clear that this introduces an element of uncertainty which would have been eliminated by the US conquest of Haiti.

The implication is this. Principle 5 requires reasonable probability of success. Given that intervention works through third parties, this is a *more* stringent requirement with respect to intervention than it is to war. Since justice in intervention, like justice in war, requires the simultaneous satisfaction of at least three principles, it is not enough for intervention to be in a just cause; it must also be a last resort, and have a reasonable prospect of success, and the evil and damage it occasions must be proportional to the end. Instances which satisfy the just cause principle are not difficult to find; there are very many circumstances in history and contemporary politics where intervention on behalf of persecuted minorities, or against corrupt and tyrannical governments would be just. Some of these could be disqualified on the grounds that armed intervention would not have been, or would not be, a last resort. But very many more, if not most, are rendered unjust by the fifth principle. The probability of successful intervention to a just end is nearly always low. Moreover, partly because this is so, there is a serious danger that the evil and damage which the intervention entails will not be proportionate to the injustice it seeks to remedy, and hence that the sixth principle will be violated also. In fact, the political circumstances where intervention seems appropriate are almost always exceedingly complex. Interventive action is accordingly usually surrounded by great difficulties and dangers. In this respect the severely limited possibilities for effective intervention in the Bosnian conflict which followed the collapse of Yugoslavia is typical. What the application of Just War shows is that such difficulties and dangers are not merely 'practical'. Practicability and morality go hand in hand.

If this is true, the principles of Just War theory amended for the purposes of regulating intervention are more successful in this respect than either an argument based on national autonomy or pure consequentialism. They will not provide a justification of the absolute ban on intervention which is the mark of contemporary international law. But they will show that the conditions which need to be satisfied if *armed* intervention is to be justified are stringent, and although the rationale involved in their interpretation and application is necessarily probabilistic, it is reasonable to think that in practice this approach to intervention will very rarely justify armed intervention. This supports the contention that non-intervention is the most defensible *norm* in international relations, and that breaking this norm can only be justified with difficulty. Arguably, this is the closest ethics can bring us to an absolute ban.

The Duty of Intervention

There is one remaining issue to be raised before we leave the topic of intervention. Suppose, in keeping with the foregoing argument, we agree that there are some rare occasions upon which armed intervention in the affairs of another country is justified. Who, if anyone, has a duty to intervene? The discussion so far has presupposed circumstances in which some country is ready and willing to intervene, the only question being whether it is justified in doing so. But there are occasions, mutual genocide in Rwanda in 1994 being one, in which no country is waiting or anxious to intervene. (In the case of Rwanda, France did eventually make a half-hearted attempt at humanitarian intervention.) Is anyone under an obligation to do so?

This question raises again a very important issue which will be mentioned here, but addressed more fully in chapter 7, namely, the moral relevance of national boundaries. If, within the borders of one country, killings on the scale which Rwanda witnessed were taking place between rival ethnic groups, no one would doubt that it was the duty of the government to do what it could to stop the carnage, and the failure to do so would rightly meet with condemnation. Why does the fact that this carnage is taking place within the borders of *another* country lessen the obligation. It is true of course, that the ability of a foreign government to act effectively is reduced in a number of ways by the fact that it is foreign, and as we have seen, this alters the ethics of intervening. But we are here considering those cases, rare no doubt, in which effective intervention in a good cause is possible. In this case it is justified. Why is it not also obligatory, as it would be within the borders of one country? Where does the parallel with the domestic case break down?

One difference, it might be replied, is that in the domestic case there is only one government whose duty it could be to act, whereas in the international case, there are many, and the duty does not obviously fall on any one of them. This is why it has often been argued that the duty to undertake humanitarian intervention falls on other states in combination, not on a single state. Often, it is alleged, there is such a duty on the international community as a whole. The issue of a duty to act in combination is another topic to be discussed at greater length in chapter 7, but for the moment, it is not difficult to see that this appeal to the community of states is not an effective reply to the point in question here. If and when it is the case that a single state *could* intervene in the affairs of another state no less effectively and to an equally good end as in its own affairs, how could its duty to do so stop at a contingent political boundary? If a neighbouring state could have halted bloodshed on the scale that it occurred in Rwanda, what morally acceptable reason could there be for thinking that it is not obliged to?

If there is an answer to this question, it must be that national borders make a moral difference. The philosophical question is whether, and how this could be so. It is a question which arises no less forcibly when we consider the relief of poverty through the redistribution of wealth, and it is in this context that it will be considered further. Before that there are further questions related to war and intervention to be considered, such as the arming of freedom fighters and the use of terrorism. These are the topics of the next chapter, and to prepare for them it will be useful to end this chapter with another summary.

Summary

International law forbids any country or group of countries to intervene in the affairs of another for any reason and by any means whatever. Sometimes this doctrine of absolute non-intervention has been defended by appeal to the autonomy of sovereign nations. This appeal rests upon a parallel with individual autonomy, one of the central concepts which structures our moral thinking. However, the extension of this idea to the nation state, even if it can be made, would not support an absolute ban on intervention, and is in fact a highly questionable parallel. An appeal to pure consequentialism does not fare much better. Although it may be able to explain why there should be a general rule against international intervention, it could not, in principle, sustain an absolute ban, since it must concede the justifiability of breaking any such rule in the rare cases where better consequences favour it.

The prospects of defending an absolute ban on intervention such as is enshrined in international law are poor, but in any case a question may be raised about the need or desirability to do so. For one thing, interventions in the affairs of other states are so common, that it may be said that the law of nations in this respect is honoured more in the breach than in the observance. For another, intervention can take many forms, some of them, diplomatic representations, for example, which could hardly have the same moral implications as others – invasion, for instance. There is reason then, to abandon the attempt to justify a rule of non-intervention and seek instead an ethic which will regulate and constrain armed intervention. Such an ethic can be formulated by adapting the principles of the Just War. Suitably amended, these can be made to generate conditions under which armed intervention is justified, and to show that these conditions are stringent enough to make the possibility of justified armed intervention relatively rare. More needs to be said, however, about the means that intervention can justifiably employ. Is it, for example, ever justified to arm terrorists in another country? This is one of the topics of the next chapter.

Suggestions for further reading

Hedley Bull, *Intervention and World Order*.
R. J. Vincent, *Non-intervention and International Order*.
Michael Walzer, *Just and Unjust Wars*, ch. 6.

6

Terrorism and Civil Conflict

Among the conclusions supported by the arguments of the last few chapters are three that set the context for the topics of this chapter. We saw first that it can be just to resort to warfare in the conduct of international relations, but that some types of war, the use of nuclear arms, for example, can never be justified because they inevitably violate the *in bello* principle of the immunity of non-combatants. We have now seen that the use of arms for the purposes of humanitarian intervention in the affairs of another country can, in principle, be justified, though probably rarely in practice. Might there be a matching restriction here too? Are there some forms of armed intervention which can also be shown to be absolutely forbidden – support for terrorist groups, for instance?

Subjectivism and the Use of Moral Language

One difficulty in the way of addressing this question is the frequent invocation of moral subjectivism in this connection. There is a familiar saying which captures this subjectivist attitude – 'one man's terrorist is another man's freedom fighter' – and its familiarity reveals the widespread adherence which relativism attracts. The idea behind the slogan is that 'terrorism' and 'terrorist' are not descriptive words. They do not pick out one sort of thing about which we might ask whether it is good or bad, but in themselves serve to condemn whatever causes and methods the user of these words happens to disapprove of. 'Terrorist' necessarily has a negative connotation, and implies condemnation. By contrast, 'freedom fighter' has a positive connotation, suggesting moral approval. What subjectivism implies is that, though both terrorists and freedom fighters use violence against the established order, whether we call them one or the other depends upon whether we disapprove or approve of that order. Those who support the established order will denounce violence against it as terrorism; those who oppose it will regard violence against it as a struggle for freedom. What this implies is that the name by which such violence is labelled does not determine our moral attitude; rather our moral attitude determines which label we choose to employ.

Moral subjectivism is an old and recurrent view in the history of ethics and philosophy. Plato argued vigorously with the subjectivists of his day, but after two and a half millennia, subjectivism, now in a variety of forms, both crude and sophisticated, continues to exercise an appeal. The issues it raises are large and complex, but we need not consider each of its ramifications here. All that concerns us is the idea that the labels 'terrorist' and 'freedom fighter' are determined not by descriptive analysis but by subjective outlook. One reason for holding this, is that people do play fast and loose with these terms in accordance with their political and other allegiances. This is true of other political terms also. For instance, the words 'democracy' and 'democratic' tend to be used, not to pick out a specific form of government which there is reason to favour, but whatever form of government the user of these words happens to favour. Similarly, terrorist groups, whose actions are condemned by governments as 'criminal', tend to refer to their own activities as 'struggle' or 'war'.

That looseness of language is a feature of political dispute and debate can hardly be denied. The more important question here, however, is whether this fact lends any support to a subjectivist interpretation of this range of political language. Looked at more closely, there is reason to think that it does not. To see this we need to ask why the use of words here takes the form it does. If the moral attitude we bring to our analysis of political conflicts is all important, those who dispute about the merits of some act of violence are not bound by the meanings of words at all. They are free to regard 'terrorist' as a term of *commendation* rather than condemnation. This is a possibility, of course. There have been a (very) few thinkers and publicists who have regarded terrorism as a positive good. The fact that those who support violently insurrectionist groups refuse to describe them as 'terrorist', and use the label 'freedom fighter' or 'guerilla', or 'revolutionary' instead, shows, not that terrorism means whatever their moral view says it means, but that, on the contrary, it has a meaning which conflicts with their moral view. Conversely, those who condemn some group as terrorist, deny them a more commendatory title because 'freedom fighter' implies a description which they think inaccurate.

'One man's terrorist is another man's freedom fighter', then, cannot really imply that we are free to use these words in accordance with our subjective interpretation. Rather, it registers the fact that violently insurrectionist groups are frequently believed by some to be terrorist, while being believed by others to be freedom fighters. Construed in this way, however, the dispute is no different to many others. People hold conflicting beliefs about a wide range of issues, and their choice of language is often an indication of this conflict of opinion. I might believe that someone is thrifty, while you believe him to be mean. But the different descriptions we apply do not merely signal our different estimations; they also give some indication of the reasons for which we hold them.

So too it is with 'terrorist' and 'freedom fighter'. To use the term 'terrorist' is not merely to condemn, but to condemn for a reason; terror is a bad thing and hence causing it is bad. To use the term 'freedom fighter' is to commend for a reason; freedom is a good thing, and hence it is commendable to fight for it.

This is not to deny that the terms 'terrorist' and 'freedom fighter' are often used carelessly. It is only to assert that they need not be, since they do have distinct meanings. Moreover, these meanings are such that, contrary to the impression given by the familiar phrase, they are not opposites. 'Terrorist' implies a means – the use of terror – while 'freedom fighter' implies an end – the struggle for freedom. To see this is to see that the means of terror could be used in the struggle for freedom and consequently, that an armed group could accurately be described as both 'terrorists' and 'freedom fighters'.

Terrorists often describe themselves as engaged in a 'war'. Equally often, this description is disputed, because to accept it seems to lend a legitimacy to their activities which those they oppose wish to deny them. So, for instance, the IRA has usually claimed to be at war, while the government of the United Kingdom has declared their activities to be criminal, and it is under the criminal law that captured IRA activists have been tried and convicted. The disagreement is an important one, but it is somewhat intractable. Members of armed groups such as the IRA not infrequently refuse to acknowledge the authority of the court, and though legal authority does not rest on the express acknowledgement of those subject to it – any petty criminal might make the same claim – disagreement about rightful authority lies at the heart of every occasion of civil conflict. It is a mistake to suppose, however, that the intractability of this dispute renders it impossible to make any headway with the moral questions that such conflict raises. We have seen in earlier chapters that the use of arms by a state whose legitimacy is not in dispute can still be unjust. It is possible, therefore, to concede the term 'war' to the violent activities of insurrectionist groups, and still to ask and answer questions about moral justification.

Freedom Fighters

Let us agree, then, that armed insurrection is war. If so, it must still satisfy the principles of Just War. These principles relate both to the aim of the insurrection and to the methods employed. In referring to insurrectionists as 'freedom fighters', we are primarily pointing to the aim that they have, and not to the methods they use. Ignoring this second issue for the moment, we may thus ask whether the pursuit of freedom is a just cause, for if it is not, gracing an insurrection with this title does not in fact secure its justification.

'Freedom' in this context is ambiguous. It might mean civil liberties, or it might mean national self-determination. A clear case of the first would be the ill-fated armed uprising in the cause of liberating the black slaves of the Southern States staged by John Brown at Harpers Ferry, Virginia, in 1859. What Brown had in view was not the establishment of a new and independent state, but the freedom of slaves within an existing one. Frederick Douglass, the champion of anti-slavery and himself a former slave, refused to join Brown's endeavour on the grounds that it was doomed to failure, and, as we have seen, this was a ground for thinking it not merely impracticable but also morally indefensible. The point however is that in this case what the *meaning* of the 'freedom' being fought for is, is clear, and I shall assume that, since slavery is a great evil, freedom in this sense is a just cause.

What is much less clear is that freedom in the sense of national autonomy is also a just cause. Of course, there have been many occasions in history when those who have taken up arms have done so against oppressive imperial forces in the belief that civil liberty and equality can only be secured by means of national autonomy. Nevertheless, the two ideas are distinct. If we think of national autonomy as government by fellow nationals (as opposed to government by foreign nationals), it is not difficult to see that such government could be as oppressive as that which it replaced, so that civil liberties were not enhanced by national autonomy. In fact, history shows that this has not infrequently been the case. The first government of the Irish Republic, for example, executed more Irishmen in five years than the British government had in twenty. But if freedom in the sense of national autonomy is neither identical with, nor any guarantee of, freedom in the sense of civil liberty, what precisely is its value? The analysis of the concept of autonomy in the last chapter threw considerable doubt upon the idea that political autonomy is really morally comparable to personal autonomy, and if it is not, this leaves us with the task of explaining what the value of political autonomy is exactly, and whether its pursuit is the pursuit of a just cause.

We do not need to answer this question here to appreciate its relevance to the topics of this chapter. The fact that there is such a question to be answered shows that it is not enough for a group to be *accurately* described as 'freedom fighters', or for the campaign in which they are engaged to be described as a 'war', to show that they are justified in their resort to arms, because they might still fail to satisfy the principle that arms must only be taken up in a just cause. The title 'freedom fighter', despite the carelessness with which it is used, does not carry automatic justification.

Suppose that we set these doubts aside and regard the struggle for freedom as a just cause (which in the case of civil liberty at least, it is). There are other principles to be satisfied before the use of arms can be justified. One of these has already been mentioned in connection with John Brown and slavery. There is no doubt that the cause in this case was just, but if Douglass was right in his estimation of the likely upshot, as he seems to have been, it still failed the test, since there was not a reasonable probability of its success. And the same might be said about many other insurrectionist causes. It can also be said of specific actions within a campaign.

Also worth considering is the proportionality principle. This states, it will be recalled, that 'the evil and damage which the war entails must be judged proportionate to the injustice which occasions it'. Now civil conflict can cause more evil and damage than wars between sovereign states. The fighting in Bosnia in the early 1990s, for example, not only produced a huge death toll, but resulted in numbers of refugees that have been matched in Europe only during World War II. Doubts about the value of national autonomy as an aim become important here again. Even granting that the pursuit of national government (Serbs ruling Serbs, Croats Croats, and so on) is a just cause, we may question whether its justice is sufficient to outweigh evil and damage on this scale. Once more, serious doubts arise about whether the bearing of arms in the name of freedom is justifiable.

Opinions will inevitably differ both on the question of the probability of success, and on the relative value of the aim in comparison to the cost of the struggle. Rational adjudication on these points is often difficult, though rarely impossible. The possibility of serious adjudication is sometimes overlooked because there is nothing very *general* to be said. For the most part, individual cases have to be considered in their particularity, and doing so requires looking at all the relevant facts. When this is actually done, the application of the principles is usually much less unclear and open to variation than is alleged.

Still, there are undoubtedly some cases where great difficulty surrounds these questions. But when this is the case, we need not be thrown into moral uncertainty, but appeal instead to another Just War principle – the principle of last resort. To make this appeal more effective, the principle of last resort needs to be combined with another moral rule, but one which has much to commend it in several other contexts. This is what might be called the rule of moral caution – it is better to lose an opportunity of acting justly than to run the risk of acting unjustly. It is not hard to think of contexts in which this rule not only applies, but is widely held. The administration of punishment is an obvious instance. In many systems of criminal law, a rule of moral caution is regarded as an important element of natural justice, generating, as it does, the principle that it is better for the innocent to go free than for the guilty to be punished. In such systems, where there is a measure of reasonable doubt about the innocence or guilt of anyone accused of a crime, it is held that he or she should *not* be convicted. Of course, if there is indeed *reasonable* doubt, then there is a good chance that the accused is guilty, and this means that the cost of applying this rule is that numbers of guilty go unpunished. Now, to fail to punish the guilty is to fail to act justly, but, the principle of moral caution holds, better this than committing a positive injustice by punishing the innocent.

To work on a principle of moral caution in the case of taking up arms, is to prefer *not* to do so whenever there is uncertainty over the value of the end and the chances of success in securing it. It is true that in refusing to take up arms, we may be failing to right a wrong, but given that taking up arms should always be a last resort, there is good moral reason to prefer to fail to right a wrong than to commit an evil.

Uncertainty over the justice of a cause and the efficacy of the use of violence, then, is not as rationally debilitating as it is often made out to be. In politics, of course, passions run high, and people will inevitably disagree profoundly. But the fact that they do disagree, does not show that from a rational point of view disagreement is unavoidable. In most cases, the principles of Just War *can* be applied with clarity and rigour, and be made to generate firm conclusions. They all constitute plausible moral requirements to make of those who would take up arms against governments, and they are stringent in the sense that they show many armed struggles to be, and to have been, morally indefensible.

Terrorism

What we have not considered so far are more precise questions about means. In the second half of the twentieth century, armed struggle has become closely associated with terrorism. But this is a contingent association, not a conceptual one. Many famous uprisings, including many successful ones, took the form of guerilla warfare, not terrorism. Castro's overthrow of the Batista regime in Cuba, for instance, was a guerilla war, not a terrorist campaign. The distinction, as we shall see, is highly relevant to questions of justification.

The debate about terrorism has tended to concentrate on the question of effectiveness. Does terrorism work? Critics of terrorism are usually keen to show, on the basis of a careful study of a variety of campaigns, that terrorism is not effective as a strategy for political ends. The evidence relevant to this debate is very extensive, however, and judgements of cause and effect in politics are difficult to make. Accordingly, a clear conclusion is hard to draw, so that if the crucial question about the rights and wrongs of terrorism is its effectiveness, it is a question which admits of no very easy answer. Fortunately, we do not actually need to know the answer to *this* question, in order to arrive at a cogent assessment of terrorism's moral merits.

Those who deny the effectiveness of terrorism seem to share with its proponents the belief that, if it does work, and if the cause in which it is employed is a good one, then terrorism is justified. Yet a campaign of violence on behalf of a just cause might work, in the sense of achieving its proponents' objective, and still be wholly indefensible, on the sorts of grounds we have just been canvassing – that the same result could have been achieved by peaceful means, or that the value of the objective is outweighed by the cost of achieving it in this way. This second objection is particularly telling in the case of the modern IRA campaign for a united Ireland, for example. The benefit of a united Ireland (if there is any benefit at all) to the people of Ireland in the late twentieth century, especially given Irish and British membership of the European Union, is tiny in comparison to the benefits that were to be expected from Irish independence in the nineteenth century. The moral case of the Fenians, the precursors of the IRA, is thus quite different to that of their contemporary successors. Whatever is to be said in defence of nineteenth-century violence on behalf of Irish independence, the aim of a united Ireland today is certainly insufficient to warrant death and destruction on the scale that a terrorist campaign involves.

So, the question of the effectiveness of terrorism is neither the sole nor the most important issue concerning its moral justification, even assuming a just cause. Indeed, even if we suppose that the other principles – last resort and proportionality – are satisfied also, we have still not concluded the debate, because it remains to consider *in bello* justice.

The use of terror is the use of a particular method. Although terrorism is commonly associated with insurrectionist groups, it is a method that governments themselves can use, both against their own citizens and against the citizens of another country. History is not short of examples. Terror consists in the causing of widespread fear and alarm by means of violence as a way of unsettling and hence controlling other people. A government which employs terror to re-inforce its control, either at home or abroad, inflicts acts of death, injury and destruction in a way that deliberately takes no account of guilt or innocence. It need not even adhere to consistency, falling randomly on loyal as well as disloyal subjects and followers. This aspect of terror is sometimes thought puzzling; surely it is more rational to reward those who are loyal. But the point of terror is to ensure that the *will* to oppose is broken, by breaking the will itself.

In this respect, the methods of terror are to be contrasted with those of martial law, however harsh a regime this may be. Military rulers may pass draconian laws to which penalties of great severity are attached, but so long as these are consistently interpreted and applied, the individual has the ability to avoid them. I may have the most serious moral objections to such laws, but I still have the choice to obey them and hence avoid retribution. Where terror rules, by contrast, wholly innocent activities, activities recognized by all to *be* innocent, may, nevertheless, result in death, injury and destruction. What marks out terror is not that it seeks to control others by force, for so also does martial law, but that it seeks to control others by making them cower in fear.

This analysis holds also for insurgents who use terrorist tactics. Whether the resort to arms is justified or not, if it takes the normal forms of war, I can (in principle) escape its rigours if I play no part in the conflict and avoid the strategic targets of either side. (In practice, nearly all wars cause innocent casualties as a side-effect.) But I cannot, even in principle, escape the tactics of a terrorist campaign. Since the purpose is to cause widespread fear and alarm among civilian as well as military populations, and the means of doing this is to distribute death and destruction in unpredictable ways, *anything* I choose to do may make me a victim of the terrorist.

In short, terror is not just a very severe or damaging use of arms, but a particular *kind* of tactic. To see that it is a tactic, however, is to see that it is not rightly described (however frequently it *is* so described) as mindless violence. It is not *mindless*, but *random*, and its randomness serves a deliberate purpose. That purpose may be a good one – to end slavery or other forms of oppression, for example – and it may be effective – the slaves are liberated, the oppressor is defeated. But for all that, it could not be a tactic employed in a Just War, because far from observing the *jus in bello* distinction between combatant and non-combatant, and respecting the immunity of the latter, terrorism precisely depends upon rendering this distinction irrelevant. If, as we saw in chapter 4, the use of nuclear weapons can be declared morally indefensible in every circumstance, so too can the use of terror.

Guerilla Warfare

This conclusion follows, of course, only if we accept the idea that the pursuit of good ends must be tempered by moral side-constraints, such as the immunity of non-combatants. In discussing the morality of nuclear weapons, we saw that this idea is called into question by consequentialist theories of right and wrong, in which a sufficiently good end always justifies whatever means achieves it. Arguments were then advanced to show that there is reason to reject consequentialism, and hence reason to reject the consequentialist criticism of Just War theory. Though these reasons did not constitute conclusive proof, it would be inappropriate to go over the arguments again. But something more needs to be said about a consequentialist approach to terrorism.

If terror can be used effectively to a good end, then it is justified. This is the consequentialist view of the matter. This way of stating it, however, omits something of significance. The most compelling debate within radical movements about tactics has nearly always been a debate about the use of violent as opposed to non-violent means. So, for example, many nationalist and liberation groups, despairing of effective change, have come to embrace violent means. Nelson Mandela records in his autobiography that the imperviousness and intransigence of the Nationalist Government of South Africa finally led him to support a campaign of violence which resulted, of course, in his conviction and imprisonment. Those who oppose violence, on the other hand, will cite Mahatma Ghandi or Martin Luther King as examples of leaders who advocated and master-minded effective non-violent campaigns, and use this as evidence that non-violence can work. What is generally clear, however, is that proponents of non-violence do not claim that it is *more* effective than violence, or that violence is to be rejected for this reason. They hold, rather that there is a *principled* objection to violence, which, whatever its efficacy, must make it a very last resort. Those who support the use of violence, on the other hand, tend to focus on effectiveness, that is beneficial consequences, but even they can generally be shown to allow that *if* a non-violent means was an effective option, it should be preferred, because the overall sum of damage and suffering would thereby be diminished.

Now, the fact that the debate among political radicals has taken this form disguises an important issue. Suppose that we conclude on the strength of the arguments presented by both sides in some specific context, that violence *is* necessary. People of good intention and peaceable disposition whose motives are unimpeachable have sometimes come to this conclusion. Frederick Douglass was such a person. Though he did not support the actions of John Brown, he did come to the view that violent action against slavery was justified because necessary. Arriving at this conclusion does not put an end to all the moral questions, however. We already know from the discussion of preceding chapters that the resort to arms, that is, to violence, *can* be justified. There still remains the question of the form of the violence. To conclude, as we are supposing, that violence is justified does not imply that terrorism is. There are other forms of armed struggle, and we might instead promote the cause of guerilla war.

Why should someone prefer guerilla war to terrorism? Just as the fundamental objection to terrorism lies in its nature, so the preference for guerilla war lies in its nature. It was noted earlier that there is often disagreement over the use of the label 'war' to describe the actions of an insurrectionist group. Those who dispute the description may do so for two different sorts of reason. They may claim that while the state under attack enjoys the political status of legitimacy, the group which uses violence against it does not, and since, properly speaking, war can only be between two parties reasonably claiming legitimacy, the violent activities of the insurrectionists cannot claim the character of war. Alternatively, or as well, it may be claimed that the tactics of the insurrectionists do not observe the rules of warfare.

Now, the first of these claims is one that has been partially dealt with already. The first principle of the Just War is that a just war can only be declared by the leaders of a state. The rationale behind this principle lies in the thought that, since war normally involves risks to large numbers of people, those who would declare war must enjoy some authority to do so. But to require that this authority is the authority of the leaders of the state, though appropriate enough in normal circumstances, perhaps, leaves the position unclear when the resort to arms is partly, sometimes wholly, occasioned by disagreements about that very authority and legitimacy. The civil wars in England, for instance, both the Wars of the Roses (1455–85) and the Civil War of 1642–6, though they involved other factors also, had this issue at their heart. To deny these the title of 'war' seems absurd, and if so, there is reason to amend the first principle of Just War in the way suggested in chapter 3. Those who would wage a just war must be able to show that they enjoy some authority, not that they enjoy the authority of a sole, lawfully recognized head of state. This is a very imprecise emendation, and could perhaps be made more precise, but the fact that some amendment of this sort is needed shows that it is *possible* for both terrorist and guerilla groups to claim a measure of legitimacy sufficient to reject this first objection.

So, it is the second claim which is of greater importance, and here there is a morally relevant distinction to be drawn between terrorism and guerilla warfare. It is simply this. Guerillas (from the Spanish 'little war') observe (many of) the rules of war. For example, whereas terrorist campaigns require that the perpetrators of acts of violence preserve anonymity, guerillas are bands of soldiers acknowledged by both sides as such. Again, the strategy of a guerilla war comprises attacks on military and related targets, not the widespread creation of fear and instability by random attacks on any and every sort of target, which is what the tactic of terrorism consists in. Guerillas, therefore, can observe these important rules of war, where terrorists cannot. It follows that there is good reason to deny terrorist campaigns the title of 'war', but more importantly, since labels in themselves are never of very great significance, the reason for doing so is that terrorism, if it cannot observe the rules of war, cannot observe them justly.

It remains to refer again to effectiveness. The common argument, as we saw, turns on whether non-violence can be as effective as the use of violence. Let us agree once more, for the sake of the argument, that calculations of cause and effect sometimes favour the proponents of violence. Any evidence mounted in support of this conclusion will not show that terrorism is more effective than guerilla warfare, for both are forms of violence. The question which of these is more effective is a different question, and a much more intractable one. This much at least can be said. Guerilla war is a more *controlled* form of violence, and for this reason we may expect it to be more effective, since it can be directed more accurately within a general strategy. This does not show that guerilla warfare must be more effective, but it does show that the onus is on those who support terrorism to prove their case. And there is good reason to think that this will be a case which is very hard to make out.

It is important to emphasize that these remarks about terrorism and guerilla warfare are not, and are not intended to be, reflections of the ways in which these words are used. Nor are they stipulative definitions. Rather, they are intended to pick out the distinguishing marks of the *concepts* of terrorism and guerilla warfare. Radical insurrectionist groups are known by many names. A guerilla army may be formed with the intention of waging open war, and end up using terrorist techniques. Those widely regarded as terrorists may also engage in guerilla warfare, which is to say, as well as deploying the techniques of terror, they may form openly recognizable armed groups whose purpose is to destroy the military resources of the state they are attacking. We are here concerned not to chart language use, but to set out the moral dimensions of, and limits on, the resort to arms, and in so doing there is a morally relevant distinction to be drawn which is embodied in the distinction between terrorism and guerilla warfare. This distinction delineates a moral possibility. Of itself it does not tell us which groups or organizations are justified in their resort to or use of arms. This is a question that can only be answered by an examination of the facts in each case. But importantly, it is the facts that determine the moral right and wrong of their activities, not the names by which they are commonly known. Conversely, of course, and this is the error which lies at the heart of subjectivism about moral language, a change of name will not alter the morality of their actions.

On the strength of this analysis, then, guerilla warfare can be justified in ways that terrorism cannot, even should it prove possible to show that terrorism is effective to a good end. Terrorism, by intention, makes victims of innocent non-combatants, and thus necessarily violates a fundamental principle of justice in the resort to arms. In short, terrorism is immoral. To arrive at this conclusion, however, is to view the moral issues surrounding terrorism from one perspective only, namely, that of those who contemplate it or engage in it. What of those whose business is to combat it?

Combating Terrorism

If terrorism is unqualifiedly immoral, are there moral limits on what we may do to combat it? The simple answer to this question is 'yes'. It is a general moral truth that those who act immorally do not thereby lose their moral status, and consequently there are ways in which it would be morally wrong to treat them. If, for example, it is absolutely wrong to enslave human beings, as I shall assume it is, it is wrong whatever the person enslaved may have done.

Those whose duty it is to combat terrorism face certain difficulties, however. In denying that terrorists are engaged in war, they bestow upon them the status of criminals, not soldiers. It follows that they are subject to the procedures and punishments of the criminal law. But to treat them in this way also gives them certain rights. In particular, it would seem, it gives them the rights which natural justice requires, the right to a fair trial, for instance. Soldiers in a guerilla army, precisely because it is an army, may be subject to attack and may be killed without inquiry. It seems that denying terrorists the status of soldiers, for all the good reasons discussed, gives them a moral protection which granting them that status would not.

The point may be made even more dramatically by considering the treatment of prisoners. The torture of enemy soldiers is forbidden by the Geneva Convention, but some defence may be mounted for the use of harsh treatment that falls short of torture for the purposes of securing information about the future plans of the enemy. Now a similar use of harsh treatment on criminals could not be justified. It is a cardinal principle of natural justice that punishments can only be inflicted for what has been done, not for what might be done in the future. If terrorists are treated as criminals, therefore, there can be no justification for treating them harshly, with an eye to the future rather than the past. Yet we know that terrorist groups will have plans which place at risk the lives and property of large numbers of innocent people. Can it be true that it is never right to treat captured terrorists in ways that would reveal these plans and hence protect the innocent?

It cannot be said that there is any very plausible solution to this difficulty. One response (it is not a solution) is to conclude that in these circumstances we have reached the limits of morality. That is to say: it is the supreme duty of the forces of law and order to protect the innocent, but it is not always possible to do so in a morally justifiable way. If so, this is one instance of what is known to philosophers as 'the problem of dirty hands'. The problem of dirty hands arises because it seems that there are occasions when politics requires what morality forbids, and effective engagement in politics in these circumstances makes it impossible to keep one's hands morally clean. In this way, something of the realism discussed in chapter 2 re-enters the discussion; the realist holds that moral scruples have no place in politics, and the argument of this chapter does seem to lend support to the suggestion that the need to combat terrorism in the real world of politics means ethical principles cannot be held to be overriding. But there is at least this difference. Realism as discussed before, espoused the *irrelevance* of morality from the outset. The realism we have now been driven to, if indeed there is no solution to the moral dilemmas that arise in the battle against terrorism, is a realism only at the extreme. It claims that on those highly unusual occasions when it is impossible to act morally, the politics of dirty hands must take over. This is consistent with the view that wherever it is *possible* to act morally and at the same time fulfil one's political responsibilities, the claims of morality are paramount. Morality is not irrelevant, but rendered inapplicable in a very few special instances.

This is, unfortunately, an unsatisfactory and untidy solution from the point of view of ethics, but it may be the best we can do. At any rate, it is the point at which the arguments of this chapter must end.

Summary

Terrorism is a major scourge of the modern world. Though it is regarded by most people as morally indefensible, there is in many quarters a sneaking sympathy where the cause in which it is employed is a just one. The analysis and arguments of this chapter show that such sympathy is misplaced. Terrorism can be shown, by its very nature, to be a resort to arms contrary to justice, and importantly different in this respect to guerilla warfare. The temptation to think otherwise arises from a mistaken concentration on the questions of the rightness of the cause and the effectiveness of means to secure it, and from a confusion over the question of the justification of the use of violent means and the justification of terrorism. By contrast, it is possible for a guerilla war to be justly declared and justly waged, though which guerilla wars are actually justified is a question that only consideration of the facts of each particular case can establish.

So much is clear. What is much less clear is what steps against terrorism are morally permissible, and whether, even, it is possible to combat terrorism both effectively and in a morally justifiable way. If it is not, this shows that there is a point at which politics must abandon moral scruple. But we can still hold that this must be the extreme and not the starting point.

Suggestions for further reading

R. G. Frey and Christopher Morris (eds), *Violence, Terrorism and Justice*. A comprehensive set of interesting essays. Loren Lomasky discusses the utilitarian/consequentialist assessment of terrorism from a fresh angle and Jonathan Glover's contribution on state terrorism is of special interest.

Ted Honderich, *Violence for Equality*. A robust defence of violence on behalf of the poor from a consequentialist point of view.

Peter Singer (ed.), *A Companion to Ethics*, relevant entry: C. A. J. Coady, 'Politics and the Problem of Dirty Hands'.

Martin Warner and Roger Crisp (eds), *Terrorism, Protest and Power*. The essays in part I are relevant to the topics of this chapter. David George, 'Terrorists and Freedom Fighters', is of special interest.

7

Poverty and Affluence

The previous chapter was concerned with the ethics of taking up arms against the state. One common reason for doing so is the pursuit of political freedom. But history shows that there is another reason, if anything more common, which motivates revolutionary groups. This is the pursuit of economic or social justice. Nationalism and the quest for national autonomy have exercised a powerful influence in modern history, but so too has socialism, whose chief interest is not so much in national liberation from foreign rule, as the liberation of the poor from grinding poverty. This cause has gathered a lot of its strength from the evident contrasts of wealth and poverty in the world, which are probably sharper now than they have ever been, because the modern world is so enriched by technological and industrial development, that its material wealth far exceeds anything that could have been dreamt of in former periods.

The disparity between rich and poor is not troublesome merely because it may give rise to violent revolution. Nor, if there is a moral problem about it, is it a problem restricted within national boundaries. There are dramatic differences in affluence and poverty *between* countries, and the demand that they be addressed is an important dimension of contemporary international relations. It provides the subject matter of this chapter, one touched upon briefly in chapter 2.

Absolute and Relative Poverty

Why is poverty a problem and what sort of problem is it? To those who look on the faces of famine these must seem strange questions. Yet they are not so easily answered. Suppose, in answer to the first, we say that poverty is a problem for the very obvious reason that it causes suffering and death. To give this answer, however, is to restrict ourselves to what is sometimes known as *absolute* poverty, as opposed to *relative* poverty.

Absolute poverty is the condition in which people have access to such limited resources that, even in the absence of illness or accident, they are constantly in danger of being unable to sustain life in the sense of continued biological existence. Now the first thing to be said about this is that absolute poverty in this sense is actually quite rare. We tend to be misled about this because of the drama of famine and the publicity that it usually attracts. When famine strikes, people are indeed without the resources to feed themselves, with the result that many die of malnutrition. But drastic famines, such as that in Ethiopia in 1984, are abnormal, and relatively unusual. They are clear and striking cases of absolute poverty, but were we to take them to be the standard of poverty as such, we would have to declare that most people in the world most of the time are not poor, that poverty is not a widespread problem. That is to say, most people most of the time are not in danger of starving or thirsting to death. (More people die from drinking (impure) water, than die from having no water to drink.)

The truth of this should not be taken to provide any consolation or to justify complacency. Human beings who are not in danger of starvation may, nonetheless, have very bad lives. And of course, when we think of the world's poor, it is not really absolute poverty we have in mind. We are thinking of people with very low incomes, whose standard of diet, housing, education, health and so on leaves much to be desired. This is revealed in the fact that evidence of poverty more often takes the form of statistics about average incomes than it does evidence of imminent starvation. So, for instance, it will be said that people in some parts of the world have an average income of, say, $10 a month. Now even allowing for differences in purchasing power and the greatly varying degrees to which different countries have cash economies, this is a very low figure. To say it is low, however, only makes sense if we are comparing it with average income in other places. The comparison is usually with the industrialized world, which used to be called 'the West', because it was largely restricted to Western Europe and the United States, but is now more frequently referred to as 'the North' because of widespread industrialization and growing prosperity in other countries north of the equator, notably in the Far East. The comparative nature of this judgement, importantly, alters the concept of poverty. We are no longer talking of absolute poverty, but of relative poverty, and this makes a moral difference.

It does so because those relatively poor in comparison with one group may be relatively rich in comparison with another. For example, compared with the inhabitants of Western Europe, many of the people of Eastern Europe are very poor. But in comparison to those of countries such as Mali or Mozambique, they are rich. Similarly, many inhabitants of Western Europe, those of Greece and Portugal, for instance, though vastly richer than those of Bangladesh, are poor in comparison to large numbers of people in North America. Facts like these leave it unclear whether *relative* poverty is automatically a matter of moral concern in the way that *absolute* poverty is.

Average income is not the only measure of well-being. Another frequently cited measure is infant mortality. But again this has to be a comparative measure. Infant mortality figures in most Western European countries have dropped dramatically over the course of the twentieth century and are now so low that they can hardly be expected to be reduced still further. Compared to these, the infant mortality figures of many of the emerging economies of the Far East are distressingly high. But they, in their turn, are far lower than those for almost all African countries. At what point should such rates cease to be of concern?

The general point to be made is this. Absolute poverty is too low a standard to set for moral concern. Relative poverty, on the other hand, is not a fixed standard at all. The description 'relatively poor' does not entail any particular state of suffering or death. It does not tell us what there is, or even whether there is anything, to be concerned about. Unless comparative disadvantage in itself is something to worry about. This is a point to which we will return.

Poverty and Cost–Benefit Analysis

Sometimes reference to the distinction between absolute and relative poverty prompts an irritated response from those who are, reasonably, exercised about the conditions in which a large proportion of the world's population has to live. As we shall see, this irritation is misplaced, but there is at least one approach to the problem which seems to side-step it. This is the approach which holds that if people are poorer than they need to be, and something can be done to alleviate their (relative) poverty, there is a moral obligation on those who can do so to act accordingly.

This is a principle similar to one endorsed by the Australian philosopher Peter Singer in an influential and widely discussed essay entitled 'Famine, Affluence and Morality', first published in 1972. Singer does not refer expressly to the distinction between absolute and relative poverty, and his argument gains some of its force from the fact that he begins with the example of the famine in East Bengal in 1971. His argument rests upon two claims: (1) that death and suffering are bad; (2) if it is in our power to prevent something very bad from happening, without thereby sacrificing anything else morally significant, we ought, morally, to do it. In illustration of this principle he gives the example of someone who can rescue a child from drowning, but only at the cost of getting his clothes covered in mud. This consideration ought not to deter, Singer argues, because the benefit greatly outweighs the cost. One of the things that Singer wishes to emphasize is the fact that this intuitively plausible principle is indifferent to spatial distance. It does not matter, morally speaking, whether the beneficiary is close at hand or far away, and from this he concludes that there is no less clear an obligation on the wealthy to eliminate poverty in countries far away than to do so within their own borders.

Singer strengthens the appeal, if not the logic, of his argument by comparing the amounts given to famine relief by wealthy countries to the amounts spent on such projects as the development of supersonic jets and opera houses. If we engage, as he suggests we ought, in a *moral* cost–benefit analysis, it is hard to see how the building of the Sydney Opera House or the development of Concorde could justifiably be preferred to the saving of lives and raising of miserable standards of living.

Singer's argument has been found highly persuasive by many. It has the great merits of clarity and simplicity and it is difficult to argue against it without seeming callous. Nevertheless, there are plausible philosophical objections to accepting it as it stands. The first of these has to do with a point made in the discussion in chapter 2 about causal relations. Singer invites comparison with a simply domestic instance – the duty on a bystander to save a drowning child. But we saw that domestic analogies cannot easily be extended to the international context. This is partly because the relations of cause and effect are more complex. As was observed before, in transferring resources from country to country, it is not merely relations between givers and receivers that come into play, but relations between systems of production and distribution. Wholesale transfer of food to famine-stricken areas (leaving aside logistical complications) can have a disastrous effect upon indigenous food production, and the same point can be made about the effect of major financial aid on local economies. Examples are not hard to find. The moral principle which Singer invokes is in fact deceptively simple. 'We ought to relieve poverty if we can do so at relatively little cost to ourselves' ignores the complexities in 'can' when we move from the domestic to the international case.

It might be thought that this objection, though important in its way, is essentially technical, and does not substantially affect the moral argument. Let us assume that this is so. There is another objection which strikes more directly at the principle he employs, and this brings us to the examination of cost–benefit analysis itself.

The relation of cost to benefit is intrinsically relative. This fact is partly disguised by Singer's choice of examples – the cost of mud-covered clothes versus the life of a child, the loss of an opera house versus the benefits of preventing starvation. In both cases, benefits of great moral significance are set against costs that seem morally inconsequential. But the relation of cost to benefit can be much closer than this and the principle still apply. Singer expresses the principle in terms of 'very bad' and 'morally insignificant'. By doing so he focuses our attention on what are in fact the extreme points of a continuous scale. But the principle would equally well apply at any two points where we could distinguish, not between 'bad' and 'insignificant', but between 'worse' and 'less significant'. In other words, cost–benefit analysis may be employed at any point on a continuum.

The point can be made most easily by the use of numbers, though of necessity these are entirely notional. Suppose the moral value of an opera house (which we will assume is a product of the pleasure it gives to the people who attend it) is 1,000 and the benefit of the lives which the sum of money it costs to build would save is 10,000,000. It is clear that morality must prefer to spend the money on saving lives. But if we change the example and replace the opera house with a morally more significant benefit, say high grade health care and secondary education for the population of a relatively small country, and give it a much closer numerical value, say 9,900,000, the moral cost–benefit principle implies that these things too must be given up in favour of relieving the poor. Alter the example again and we can see that, taken to its logical conclusion, the principle implies that we are obliged to give assistance up to the point at which we are only fractionally better off than those to whom we give it. In short, Singer's principle requires not merely sacrifice of those things we might regard as luxuries or inessentials, such as opera houses and supersonic travel, but *maximum* sacrifice of highly valuable benefits in favour of the most marginal gain. To many minds this renders it a much less plausible principle than at first appears. The trouble lies in the fact that it requires us to regard relative poverty in the same way that we regard absolute poverty; we must sacrifice highly significant benefits if this would make people who are poorer than us, but not specially poor, marginally better off. If the price of being morally in the right is as high as this, however, we may wonder why, and whether, morality has an overriding call upon us at all. One thing is certain, if the principle of maximum sacrifice really is the logical implication of moral arguments for foreign aid, it is not an argument that will as a matter of fact command the allegiance or compliance of governments.

This objection to Singer's argument does not constitute a complete refutation. Someone persuaded of the cost–benefit approach and with a very robust attitude might accept that morality does require maximum sacrifice. There are two other objections still to be brought, however. The first is that moral cost–benefit analysis requires measurements that cannot be made. The numbers used to illustrate the full force of the principle were entirely notional. But could meaningful values ever be attached to the possible courses of action over which cost–benefit analysis is supposed to range? There are at least two difficulties here. One relates to the open-endedness of the necessary valuations. Take the case of opera house versus lives saved from starvation again. To compare the two it seems we need to know things it is impossible to know – on the one hand, how long the opera house will last, what the average attendance will be and how much pleasure those attending derive from it, and on the other, how long those who are saved will live, and what the quality of their lives will be. The second difficulty relates to comparability. Can we really compare the value of the pleasure of opera going with the continued existence of a peasant farmer? Singer says: 'When we buy new clothes not to keep ourselves warm but to look "well-dressed" we are not providing for any important need.' His argument rests heavily upon judgements such as these, but can they be made and how are they to be defended?

Philosophical opinion differs on how important these difficulties are. It has to be agreed, I think, that such values cannot be *quantified*. There are no real numbers we can use, and this has inclined some people to think that any comparison is impossible.

But it is clear that quantification is not essential; qualitative comparison is enough. To take a simple case. I can meaningfully say that, though I am partial to both, I like ice-cream better than chocolate, without any suggestion that I could put numbers to my preference. Similarly, I can say with perfect propriety that it is morally more important for me to take my aunt to hospital than to return a borrowed book, without being committed to quantifying the relative strength of my obligation. Looking well dressed is important, but, generally speaking, it is not as important as staying warm. And so on. The subject of comparing values is more complicated than these simple examples suggest, but the fact that such judgements are a familiar and intelligible part of everyday life gives us good reason to think that the idea of comparison which cost–benefit analysis requires is not in fact impossible.

A more significant objection is this. The argument we have been considering assumes that the action of distributing benefits more equally will not itself alter the benefits to be distributed. The picture in mind is something like the division of a cake into more rather than less equal parts. However we divide it, the size of the cake remains the same. But this is not the case with the division of the world's resources. Such at least is one of the contentions of another highly influential essay.

Lifeboat Ethics

'Lifeboat Ethics: The Case Against Helping the Poor' is the title of an essay by Garrett Hardin. In it he compares the world to a lifeboat and its population to the people who are both in it and trying to get in. Hardin's point is that the carrying capacity of a lifeboat is limited. Those who are in it are more fortunate than those who are not, but it would be a mistake to think that this good fortune can be extended to all those who would claim a place, because the more people who board it, the smaller the chance that it will save any. In other words, sharing the benefit has an effect on the benefit to be shared, and at the extreme, sharing the benefit eliminates it altogether.

Hardin uses the image of the lifeboat to draw conclusions about the distribution of the world's resources. In doing so he draws another parallel – what is known as the 'tragedy of the commons'. Common grazing land is a benefit, but it is so only so long as the number who can use it is limited. Put enough animals on it, and the grazing is destroyed, with the result that no one gains any benefit. Not only do those who gain admission derive no advantage; those who formerly generated a living from it lose what they had. The net effect of sharing, consequently, is not a better life for people who were poor, but a worse life for all, and in the limiting case, the death of all.

The parallel with the world at large is not hard to draw. Those whom the world sustains at a tolerable level of living might, following Singer's argument, suppose that they can, and have an obligation to, share their good fortune as widely as possible. But this belief rests upon the false supposition that sharing will not diminish the good fortune. It will, and it can do so disastrously. The picture is a simple one. To take the image of the cake again. If the division is extensive enough, the slices become vanishingly small to the point where they are too small to sustain anyone. If Hardin's reasoning is sound, it is not hard to see its moral import. While it might seem both selfish and callous for those in the lifeboat to refuse to take on board others who otherwise will evidently drown, not to do so is to ensure that all are lost instead of some. Similarly, in considering the distribution of the world's resources, it cannot be right to accept a principle whose application, far from increasing human welfare, would eliminate it altogether.

Moral reasoning which relies too heavily on metaphors and images is always questionable. In considering Hardin's argument it is interesting to note that though it leads to a conclusion diametrically opposed to Singer's it shares a common assumption. This is the assumption that the capacity of the lifeboat, and of the commons, is fixed. Hardin sees, rightly in my view, that the fact that a resource is of a certain size does not imply that whatever way we divide it the benefit remains the same. It is plainly correct that if the shares of any resource are small enough, they cease to be of any benefit. What is incorrect is the assumption that the world's resources are fixed.

That the world's population is growing, and growing in roughly geometrical proportions cannot be seriously doubted. There are many more people now than ever before in the world's history, and the period of time it takes for the population to double has diminished rapidly over the last 150 years. These facts have led very many people, and governments, to the conclusion that population control is crucial to the future well-being of humankind because of what Paul Ehrlich has termed 'The Population Bomb'. In arriving at this conclusion they presuppose that an expanding population, at least one expanding at current rates, is unsustainable because it represents an increasing drain on resources. In turn this implies that an expanding population cannot increase resources. This presupposition and its implication can be questioned, however, and have been questioned by, amongst others, the economist, Julian Simon, in whose opinion the discussion of population growth has been distorted by 'An Oversupply of False, Bad News', the title of another important essay.

There is a slogan coined by those who are resistant to policies of population control: when God sends another mouth he also sends another pair of hands. This slogan has come in for considerable ridicule from those persuaded of the reality of the population 'bomb'. But it expresses an important truth. People are not merely consumers; they are also producers, and not only producers but inventors. Human work and ingenuity can turn the valueless into the valuable, and in this way dramatically *increase* the world's resources. Hardin's picture is one of resources which can only be depleted by additional people, whereas an increase in population can extend them.

A good illustration of this is oil. The oil which has made such a huge difference to food production, heating and transport in the twentieth century was utterly useless until human ingenuity found ways to retrieve it and use it. In other words it *became* a resource. Now, of course, oil, like coal and iron ore and many other valuable materials is a finite resource. We do not know, even yet, just how much there is, but we know that the supply is not infinite. This is why people often think that ways must be found to switch to *renewable* resources. But there is a fallacy in reasoning from the finitude of a particular resource such as oil to the finitude of resources. Just as oil became a resource through human inventiveness, so other substances and techniques which are now useless will become useful. While it is true in the abstract that all resources, even renewable ones are finite, it is also true that resources are indefinitely large.

That *more* people can mean *richer* people and not poorer people, is demonstrable. It is estimated that the population of California is 45 times larger now than it was when the Spaniards first arrived there, yet the people of California are among the richest in the world and vastly better off than the scattered tribes of native Americans who populated California in the sixteenth century. Though the calculation is almost impossible to work out, it seems likely that a similar point could be made about the world as a whole.

The image of the lifeboat is inappropriate as a metaphor for the world, because it implies that the resources of the world are not only finite, but definite, that is, ascertainable. The two are not the same. Something can be *indefinitely* large without being *infinitely* large. For any lifeboat, we can tell how many people it will take before it sinks. The world's resources, by contrast, though they are not infinitely large, are indefinitely large. There is no ceiling to them that we can ascertain, and this indefiniteness is, in part, a result of expanding population.

Hardin's metaphor is misleading in another way as well. The benefit of being in the lifeboat is the same for all who secure it – their lives are saved instead of lost. The benefit accruing from the same share of material resources, on the other hand, can vary according to the person receiving it. This possibility is a result of what economists know as 'marginal utility'. The law of marginal utility states that the more one has of a good the less benefit one derives from still more of it. Conversely, the less one has of a good, the more one benefits from more of it. For instance, if I have a monthly income of $10, an increase of $1 a month is of considerable value. If I have a monthly income of $10,000 an increase of $1 is not of any very great value. In other words, from the point of view of usefulness it is not true that a dollar is a dollar.

It follows from the existence of marginal utility that the way in which material resources are distributed can alter the degree to which they are beneficial. Hardin is correct in his belief that the way in which a given resource is divided can diminish its beneficial value. What he overlooks is the fact that it can increase it also. Moreover, the rate of increase is itself increased once we add productive creativity to marginal utility. A resource may be more productive if given to one user than if given to another. This is one of the thoughts behind campaigns for intermediate technology. A given sum of money spent on raising low-level technology to a slightly higher level (wooden to metal ploughs, for instance) can make a large difference to productivity, where the same sum of money spent on trying to raise high-level technology to still higher levels would result in no increase in productivity at all.

The conclusion has to be that the lifeboat analogy not only fails to be illuminating; it is seriously misleading in thinking about issues of world population and wealth distribution. The possibility of a 'tragedy of the commons' is indeed a reason to question simple cost–benefit analysis, but making this possibility central to the argument does no better in enabling us to make progress with the topic of poverty and affluence.

Taking Stock of the Arguments

The discussion which has brought us to this point has been somewhat complex. It is therefore advisable to pause in order to take stock of the arguments and see what line of thought it would be most promising to pursue next.

Neither Singer's simple principle of doing good to others nor Hardin's alternative 'lifeboat' approach to the problem of the world's poor has proved convincing. Both may be described as 'general welfare' arguments. Singer thinks that if the rich were to share their resources with the poor there would be an increase in well-being, and that this creates an obligation on them to do so. Hardin thinks that radical redistribution of goods will actually lead to a diminution in general well-being and that, however harsh it may sound, helping the poor is for this reason to be resisted. Both positions, however, fail to take full account of the fact that the world's wealth is not to be thought of as a vast storehouse which is distributed this way or that. The things that nature provides are valuable only in so far as they are usable to human ends, and their conversion from mere materials to genuine resources is a result, in large part, of creative productivity. Moreover, not only do the processes of creativity and production alter the value of the 'goods in store', so too does the way in which they are distributed. In short, questions of distribution cannot be separated from questions of general welfare.

This point, it seems to me, by rendering Hardin's metaphor inappropriate, robs his argument of its force. But it does not damage Singer's case quite so seriously. Indeed it could be construed as strengthening it because, if it is true that a more equitable distribution of goods would increase their value, there is even more reason, on Singer's premises, to suppose that this implies an even stronger obligation to undertake it.

What this means, in effect, is that the central problem with Singer's argument is that, taken to its logical conclusion, it implies maximum sacrifice, the giving up of everything to the point where we are only fractionally better off than those we are helping. Sometimes it has been argued that considerations of practicality cause us to advance a version of the principle which falls short of this extreme. If the idea of moral argument is to influence people's behaviour for the better, any recommendation which is unlikely to command compliance is to this extent a moral failure. Since we can be pretty sure that almost no one will actually be persuaded to make a maximum sacrifice, we therefore have reason, from a moral point of view, to recommend moderate if not minimal sacrifice.

This response is not altogether satisfactory. If Singer is right, we ought to be prepared to make a maximum sacrifice. This is what morality requires of us. How then can the fact that we, along with most people, *will* not do so, make it right that we *should* not? But this is what the recommendation of a principle of moderate sacrifice implies. It seems that the appeal to practicality, in fact, implies a contradiction. The original argument tells us that we are obliged to make maximum sacrifice, while the modified principle, treated as an alternative moral recommendation, tells us that we are not.

Even if there is some way out of this difficulty, there is another problem. If we go for the moderate version, what is to motivate us is concern with doing good to the degree that we are prepared to do it. Those to whom we give (some proportion of) our resources, though it is to be hoped that they will benefit, are mere passive recipients of a level of largesse which we ourselves decide. Singer claims that his argument undermines the traditional distinction between charity, the things we do out of generosity, and duty, the things we ought to do. By a curious route, however, the distinction may be thought to have been undermined in the wrong way. Certainly, a different way of viewing the problem is to say not that we have a duty to give to the poor, but that the poor have a right to be given to. This, though, shifts the whole argument, for it appears that the relief of poverty thus becomes not a matter of welfare, but of justice.

Social Justice and Welfare Rights

Whatever conclusion we reach in the end on this important subject, it is certainly true that many people regard the disparity between affluence and poverty in the modern world as a striking instance of injustice. The topic of social distributive justice is one of the most widely discussed in contemporary moral and political philosophy. The literature it has generated is enormous, but it has not produced any very widespread consensus about either the concept itself, or what it implies for social policy. The idea of distributive justice generates special problems when applied to the realm of international relations, and since this is our prime con-

cern here, it will be sufficient to rehearse briefly some of the
more general problems involved in thinking clearly about it.

People often conflate justice and equality, but it is fairly easy to
show that the two are distinct. Unjust distribution is not the same
as unequal outcome. Suppose, for instance, that two people freely
enter a lottery with equal stakes. One wins the jackpot, say $1
million, and the other the minimum prize, say $10. There is a
gross inequality of outcomes, but this is no reason to conclude
that there has been injustice. To claim that there had been, we
would need to show that something had gone wrong in the
process leading to this outcome. The same point may be made of
other circumstances. Two people set up in business under conditions of open competition. One thrives, the other fails. Again
there is a dramatic inequality of outcome, but no reason to think
it unjust. Nor does distributive justice have any very clear connection with desert. A student may work extremely hard for an
examination but, having no aptitude for the subject, fails. Another student works much less hard, but being more able, passes.
In circumstances so described, we might say that the first student
deserved to pass, but the examiners cannot be accused of injustice
in the fact that he or she did not.

Equality does have a role to play in these cases, but it is not
equality of outcome. The lottery must give an equal chance to
both tickets, the examiners must apply the same standard equally
to both candidates. Equal treatment, however, is consistent
with unequal outcomes. This suggests an important problem for
thinking about poverty and affluence in terms of justice. What
is troublesome about poverty is the suffering and deprivation
it brings with it, but if a fair and equal system can result in
deprivation, the problem of deprivation, it seems, cannot be a
problem of injustice.

One solution to this puzzle is the concept of a welfare right.
Whereas most rights are generated by specific actions – rights
bestowed by contracts, for instance – a welfare right is a right to
a basic level of welfare which we acquire not by virtue of
something we have done or others have agreed to, but simply by
virtue of the condition we have fallen into. An example would
be this. Imagine that in some remote part of the country each

household depends for water on its own well. Geological factors might determine that the supply of water varies somewhat, and one household might agree to pay another for additional water to provide for, say, a swimming pool. Having paid for the water, they have a specific right to it. But in extreme circumstances, where a well has dried up and a family has not even water for drinking, they are said to have a general welfare right to a share of the water in other wells. This right derives not from any agreement they have reached but from their pressing need. The need to fill my swimming pool is not basic; the need of water to drink and wash is.

The concept of a welfare right is not accepted by all social philosophers, but the reasons they have for challenging it are not of primary interest here. More interesting for present purposes is this question. Against whom do those in need have this right? The householder who makes an agreement to buy additional water from another householder, has a right against that house-holder. But if his well dries up, and there are several other functioning wells in the neighbourhood, against whom does he have the welfare right for water? The answer is, no one in particular, and what seems to be required if such welfare rights are to be met is a *general* system of welfare insurance, to which all contribute in some fair and equitable way. This is the thinking behind redistributive taxation whose purpose is to guarantee a minimum social provision, a safety net through which no one falls, however badly their lives may go.

At one level it seems plainly in everyone's interest that there be such a system, for no one knows when they may fall on hard times. Yet there is a curious paradox here. Though it is in my interest that there *be* such a system, it is also in my interest that if there is, I do not contribute to it, that I should, in the language of political philosophy, be a 'free-rider'. If everyone else contrib-utes and I do not, I am at an advantage. If everyone else does not, and I do, I am at a disadvantage. So *either* way, it is in my interests not to contribute. But what is good reasoning for me is equally good reason for everyone else. Consequently, while it is in everyone's interest not to contribute, it is also in everyone's interest that there be such a system. This is what is called 'a co-ordination problem', and the solution to it lies in having a sovereign power which can *compel* everyone to contribute. This is one argument (an application of Hobbes's theory of the state, in fact) for the necessity of a state with coercive powers.

Welfare rights, then, are rights against everyone else. The only way in which they can be protected is by a compulsory system of contribution, and it is one of the duties of the state to ensure that there is such a system. It should be noted that there are important difficulties and complexities associated with this line of reasoning, and a number of philosophers think that many of these are, in fact, insuperable. Assuming that they can be overcome, however, the point to stress is that this argument for welfare rights accords a central role to the state. In extending the concept of welfare rights to an international· context, therefore, we encounter a problem which has recurred several times throughout this book — the absence of an international super-state.

Basic Rights and National Boundaries

Within a single state, welfare rights can be set at a variety of levels. We might institute, as most welfare states do, rights for all citizens not merely to basic levels of food, clothing and shelter, but to a minimum level of education and health care. In the context of world poverty, concern tends to be focused on chronic deprivation and for this reason it is customary to speak not of welfare rights, associated as they are with the idea of the welfare state, but 'basic' rights, the claims of any human being to protection in the face of wholly debilitating poverty. Just what level of maintenance basic rights entitle people to, is, of course, a different, and difficult question, but we can assume that it will be set above that of absolute poverty without being indefinitely relative.

Now, the same problem arises over basic rights as welfare rights more generally considered. A right is of no value unless someone has an obligation to supply the thing to which it is a right. Against whom are these 'basic' rights held? Who has the obligation to see that they are satisfied? It is the duty of each state to ensure a system of welfare rights for its own citizens. The problem of world poverty arises because there are some countries too poor to provide a welfare system. Yet if it must be accepted that there are many countries in which large numbers of people fall short of basic rights, it is also evident that there are a good number of countries whose wealth is sufficient to provide them. But which of these countries is under an obligation to do so? To repeat: it is the duty of each state to ensure a system of welfare rights for its own citizens. This implies nothing about duties to those who are not its citizens. The duty of the state in this respect seems to stop at national boundaries.

One obvious answer is that the obligation to meet the basic rights of inhabitants of poor countries falls on *all* prosperous nations, collectively, and indeed wealthy countries might agree to co-operate in providing assistance to the poor. It needs to be observed, however, that such co-operation could not be based on Hobbesian grounds. Since there is no prospect whatever that the USA, for example, could come to be as in need of assistance from Mali as the other way about, it cannot be said to be in the interests of the USA that there be a worldwide system of wealth redistribution.

Something of the same sort might be said about the domestic case, of course. In any prosperous country there will be individuals whose chance of falling on truly hard times is remote in the extreme, and it is not any more in *their* interests that there should be a system of welfare rights. Still, it is in the interests of the majority, and equity requires the state to compel *all* citizens to contribute to the burden of providing it. This goes to show that the problem in the international arena is, once more, the absence of a sovereign power.

There are two ways in which the argument about world poverty can proceed. If we take the case for universal basic rights to have been made out, and further hold that they can only be upheld by an institution with the power and authority to create and maintain an international welfare system, we can construe the disparities of affluence and poverty which mark the modern world as a strong argument for world government. Among the things to be said against this, however, is its unreality. If the solution to world poverty lies only with the introduction of world government, in reality this amounts to saying that there is no solution, since the prospect of a world government with effective international powers equivalent to the domestic powers of the nation state is almost nil.

Those persuaded by the argument might refuse to accept this counsel of despair. It is, after all, only a prediction. Who is to say that world government is only a remote possibility? And who is to say that it cannot be made less remote by pressing the case of the poor? Unfortunately, in addition to this point about unreality, there seems to be an important hiatus in the argument. Recall that the equivalent domestic argument relies upon most people having a plausible need for insurance against hard times. Very few people, if any, can be quite sure that they will not be struck by accident, illness or unemployment. This is the background condition that makes it in their interest to agree to a compulsory welfare system. But whole countries are not subject to such things, except in a metaphorical sense, and so the Hobbesian argument cannot apply in the same way. It is not just that world government is unlikely to come about. The rationale for bringing it about is lacking also.

An alternative line of thought lies in accepting that the only motivation for international relief of poverty lies in good will. People have a right to basic necessities, and many people in the world's poor countries lack them, while those in affluent countries have them in abundance. Although it cannot be shown that any one wealthy country, or group of countries, has the responsibility of recognizing these rights, moral decency requires that at least something should be done, and countries alive to the claims of morality thus have a reason to act. Their duty to do so is limited, however. No one country, or even group of countries, can be shown to have a duty to meet every claim to basic rights, something which is probably impossible in any case. The duty to act is what moral philosophers call an *imperfect* duty. A *perfect* duty may be defined as one which it is always wrong to act contrary to. Thus telling the truth is, arguably, a perfect duty, since we should always act in accordance with it. Charitable giving, by contrast, is an imperfect duty, for while it is wrong never to act in accordance with it, it is morally permissible not always to be doing so. If I *never* give to charity, I am failing in my duty, but at any given moment I may, permissibly, be omitting to do so.

To think of the matter in this way has the philosophically interesting implication that the poor can have a right to relief, while those who fail to respond in any given instance are not acting unjustly. The relation of poverty to affluence *is* thus a matter of rights, but *not* of justice.

International Charity

The traditional virtue of charity has fallen on hard times. It no longer has a morally respectable image, and this is partly why talk of charity has been replaced by talk of rights and justice. If the arguments of this chapter are correct, however, the fact that the world's poor have a basic right to assistance does not remove the need for the charity of the rich. On the contrary, if charitable motivation is not a morally worthy ground upon which to base assistance, there appears to be no other ground. Perhaps then we should enquire whether charity deserves the poor opinion in which it now tends to be held.

One objection to charitable giving is that it necessarily implies an inequality between given and receiver. In one respect, of course, there is indeed inequality – the givers are rich and the receivers are poor. If there were not this inequality, there would be no problem in the first place. But no further implication of inequality need follow. In giving to the poor, we need not regard them as inferior in any other sense, and indeed, it is plausible to think that the motivation to give is most intelligibly rooted in a belief in their being fellow human beings with similar needs and desires, arising from a common vulnerability to what the Book of Common Prayer calls 'the changes and chances of this fleeting world'. Charity can be the expression of belief in a shared humanity.

A second objection is that charity gives rise to dependence on 'handouts'. Now it is true that good intentions can lead to undesirable results, and that this has happened in international relief programmes. But the connection between charity and dependence is a purely contingent one. Charitable assistance does not *have* to take the form of simple handouts. Since the establishment of worldwide organizations like Oxfam, a great deal has been learnt, and the strategy of 'helping people to help themselves' in sustainable development programmes has widely come to be preferred over simple 'relief', except in cases of abnormal famine or disaster. A belief in charity is the conviction that morality requires us to assist, not that we should assist in some particular fashion, and intelligence and imagination, if they have sometimes been lacking on the part of relief organizations in the past, are wholly compatible with charitable motivation.

A third objection to charity springs from a quite different source, namely the belief that charitable assistance, by ameliorating the worst aspects of poverty, diminishes the political pressures which would impel a radical revolution of the social order which generates it. Behind this objection there is a large and ambitious economic theory, for the most part Marxist, which encompasses an explanation of the causes of poverty, the need for revolution and the way in which it can be brought about. All these are large topics, which there is not space to investigate here. It is worth noting, nonetheless, that the plausibility of Marxist theory and the socialist ideal has diminished considerably in recent times, largely because of historical experience. The sort of revolution, if such is possible, which would radically improve the lot of the poor is as far away as ever, and consequently to deny them charitable assistance, albeit of a limited sort, is to deny them any improvement whatever. This could only be an appealing conclusion to those who do not themselves suffer very much from the rigours of deprivation.

These relatively brief remarks suggest that the tarnished image which the idea of charity has come to have may be unwarranted. More importantly, there is a more positive point to be made. We saw that the approach to poverty which construes it in terms of a basic right which distributive justice requires to be satisfied encounters a major problem in the context of international affairs; there is no international government to implement this justice, and the redistributive obligations of national governments stop at their own frontiers. If assistance to the poor of this world is grounded in charity, however, these problems fall away, because while it is true that truly charitable assistance to poor countries plays a very small part in the foreign policy of most nations, the obligation of charitable assistance is not restricted to states and governments, but applies just as much to moral agents as individuals.

That this is widely recognized is borne out by the huge expansion that has taken place in the number and size of voluntary organizations devoted to international relief. The medium- to long-term effectiveness of these non-government organizations, or NGOs as they are generally known, is hard to assess, but there are at least two reasons for thinking that the assistance of NGOs is *more* effective in *better* ways than that of government-to-government aid. First, the problems of poor countries are in many cases compounded by corrupt and inefficient government. Although some state aid is channelled through NGOs, aid *from* states is generally aid *to* states and this means a gap opens up between the recipient of assistance and the people by whom it is needed. Poor countries are rarely uniformly poor, and aid from wealthy states, which is intended to relieve the lot of the worst off, with depressing frequency ends up in the hands of the indigenous rich. Second, very few wealthy countries resist the temptation to tie the giving of aid to other concerns. A large proportion of what appears in the advertised list of aid projects is military, or connected with trade agreements, or political alliances. These motives can assist in the increase of local prosperity, but when they are the sole, or even principal motivation, their continuing to do so is uncertain.

This much is clear. It is largely charitable motivation that has led to the creation of NGOs whose achievements are real, and in the evident absence of better, we should take satisfaction in a moral argument which shows that motivation to be as well grounded as any other, and better than most.

Summary

Poverty is a major problem in very many countries, and one intensified in many eyes by the widening contrast with the ever-increasing affluence of others. To formulate the moral structure of this problem adequately is not as easy as it might appear. Appealing to the desirability of doing good at relatively insignificant cost is deceptively simple, but a response which urges us to resist the impulse to share lest we reduce all to penury is equally ill founded. It is plausible to think that all human beings have certain basic rights, and consequently those who have more than enough are under an obligation to help those who have not. There is an important disanalogy between the national and the international context, however. While in the former we can construct an argument which shows the justice of a system of welfare rights enforced by the state, the absence of world government makes this inapplicable to the latter. If basic rights are to be met, they have to be recognized out of a sense of charity, not justice, and despite the poor image that charity often has, this is, in fact, as good a moral grounding for the relief of the poor as can be constructed.

Suggestions for further reading

W. Aiken and H. Lafollette (eds), *World Hunger and Moral Motivation*. The essays by Hardin and Singer will both be found in this volume.

C. R. Beitz, *Political Theory and International Relations*, part III.

Gordon Graham, *The Idea of Christian Charity*. An exploration and defence of the virtue of charity in a theological context.

L. Gruen and D. Jamieson (eds), *Reflecting on Nature*. This collection includes a section on population and consumption, including extracts from Ehrlich and Simon.

Onora O'Neill, *The Faces of Hunger*. An argument for relief of poverty based on the Kantian conception of duty rather than utility or justice.

Henry Shue, *Basic Rights*. A comprehensive treatment of many of the ideas explored in this chapter.

Peter Singer (ed.), *A Companion to Ethics*, relevant entry: Nigel Dower, 'World Poverty'.

8

The Politics of
the Environment

International ethics is sometimes referred to as 'global ethics'. This label is part descriptive and part revisionary. In its descriptive sense 'global ethics' is meant to convey the idea that certain ethical concerns apply globally, not just within the borders of one country or even one culture, that moral principles do not stop at national boundaries. In its revisionary sense, 'global ethics' is more ambitious. It carries the implication that to take seriously the idea that we are inhabitants of one world means accepting that a wholly new approach to moral questions is required.

Although a number of problems and developments have generated this idea – international telecommunication systems, worldwide travel on a vastly increased scale, international terrorism and the proliferation of nuclear weapons – there is little doubt that the greatest impetus to the idea of *global* ethics is an increasing awareness of environmental issues. The purpose of this chapter is to explore some of these issues with a view to asking whether they really do require a radical reappraisal of ideas, one which will lead to a new politics of the environment.

Ecology and Environment

In 1993 a conference popularly known as 'The Earth Summit' was held in Rio de Janeiro and attended by representatives of almost every nation in the world. Two beliefs led to the calling of this conference: that the earth faces a common crisis, and that it is in the interests of all to join together in combating it. The first of these beliefs owes much to increasing scientific knowledge about changing climatic conditions and the effect of human processes upon them. One such change dominated many of the headlines, namely global warming.

This is the hypothesis that the mean temperature of the planet is rising. Most parts of the world experience changes in temperature between the seasons – from hot in summer to cold in winter to hot in summer again, and so on. But the range within which these changes take place – from the hottest summer temperature to the coldest winter temperature – is not fixed, and the thesis of global warming is that the range is moving upwards.

A change in this range can be very small, and still have considerable effect on local climates. Changes in local climates – variations in seasonal temperatures and rainfall – in turn have an effect on vegetation and thus on animal life. In so doing, of course, they also change the agricultural conditions, and hence the production of food. It is at this point that we arrive at the implications of global warming for human beings, though the connection with human life is to be found at the beginning of the chain also.

One explanation of global warming is the huge increase in the emission of carbon dioxide through industrial and commercial processes. We should think of fossil fuels – oil, coal and so on, as well as wood, as repositories of century upon century of carbon dioxide extracted by plants from the atmosphere. These stores have been laid down over an extremely long period of time, and what the use of coal, oil and wood in large quantities does is to release this carbon dioxide in a very much shorter time. Carbon dioxide goes on being withdrawn from the atmosphere by vegetation, but the rate at which it does this is far slower than the rate at which it is released again by combustion. Furthermore, as the forests of the world are depleted (in part to provide fuel), the rate at which carbon dioxide is withdrawn, slow as it naturally is, is made even slower. The effect of industrialization, therefore, is to precipitate a large-scale change in the composition of the atmosphere.

The connection with temperature is this. Carbon dioxide is a 'greenhouse' gas. That is to say, its presence in the atmosphere has an effect similar to that of the glass in a greenhouse; it lets the warmth of the sun in, but retards its escape, and thus causes the area below it to warm up. The more carbon dioxide, the greater the retardation, and so the temperature on earth rises. The longer-term effects of this rise could be dramatic. A huge amount of water is held at the Poles in the form of ice and snow. A sufficient rise in temperature could cause a proportion of this to melt, with the further consequence of a substantial rise in sea level. A rise in sea level means the submergence of land, and on some predictions the land likely to be submerged would include heavily populated areas, containing within them whole cities.

Not so long ago, the idea that the operation of a factory in Europe could have consequences for tropical rain forests, or that my driving to work could contribute to widespread flooding in distant countries, would have seemed far fetched. Nowadays, the postulation of such connections is commonplace. This change in thinking is owed to ecology. Ecology is the study of interconnected systems, and such studies can be conducted for quite small ecosystems. An ecological study of a lake, for instance, is concerned to reveal the interconnectedness of vegetation, insects, fish, birds and mammals. According to standard ecology (what is known as 'new' ecology takes a different approach) such a system will normally exhibit an equilibrium, a condition in which all these various facets of its life are in balance – the populations of insects, fish and birds are such as to maintain each other. Temporary disturbances in an ecosystem are continuous. Weather of a certain type, for instance, may cause the number of insects to increase, which will for a time sustain an increased number of fish, and then the number of predatory birds. But as the numbers of fish increase, the number of insects diminishes, and as the birds increase the fish diminish, until equilibrium is reached again.

In contrast to these normal temporary disequilibria, which right themselves, there can also be major disturbances, which alter the balances so significantly that the equilibrium cannot be restored, and a sequence of changes is begun which ends in a different equilibrium where the organisms of the system are balanced in quite different proportions. Pollution of a lake with pesticides, say, by killing large numbers of fish, because of consequent effects on other life forms, will alter the system radically, so that it cannot return to its original equilibrium.

Ecological study can, in principle, be extended to larger and larger systems. Taken to its limit it allows us to view the whole globe as an ecosystem, which also has its balance, and it is this way of viewing it which has brought to attention the possible consequences of large-scale human effects. Global warming is a prime instance, but others widely discussed are acid rain and the effects on the ozone layer. All three are examples of local processes having long-distance and long-term effects of far greater significance than surface appearances would lead us to expect. In short, ecology has transformed our understanding of the world in which we live, and alerted us to hitherto unimagined dangers.

Ethics and Environmental Crisis

What exactly are the ethical implications of this? A whole new branch of moral philosophy has sprung up under the name of environmental ethics, or more generally environmental philosophy. Some of the topics discussed under this heading are not in fact new. The rights and wrongs of our treatment of animals, for example, has quite a long history, and, as we saw in the last chapter, the ethics of population growth and the use of natural resources has an important part to play in the discussion of social or distributive justice between nations. But what is new, or believed to be new, is the need to consider questions of moral responsibility and political organization in a global context, hence the other label 'global ethics'.

The sense of a need to think afresh about questions of ethics in international relations gains much of its stimulus from the belief that ecology has alerted us to a potential (some would say *pending*) crisis of, literally, earth-shaking proportions. The idea is simple enough. Hitherto our concern has been with issues conditioned by national boundaries – self-determination of peoples, rules of war, nuclear deterrence, transnational obligations to the poor. But environmental disaster is no respecter of political divisions. The time seems to have come, therefore, when such issues should be set aside in favour of tackling a huge, and *common*, threat.

It is worth stressing that the prospect of crisis plays a large part in the demand for a radical re-thinking of moral parameters. If the problems to which ecology appears to have alerted us were more modest, they could be subsumed (along with the other issues we have been discussing) under the familiar concepts and arguments – rights versus welfare, broadly – which have been the long-standing currency of international relations. The protection of political sovereignty and the promotion of mutually advantageous trade, pales to insignificance in comparison with flooding and famine on a global scale. In the face of less pressing problems, however, these issues retain the importance they have always been thought to have. Consequently, in order to assess the true novelty of environmental ethics, we need to ask about the basis of the belief in crisis.

In elaborating the idea of global warming I was careful to describe it as a *hypothesis*. This is what it is, in fact, despite the tendency in some quarters to speak as though it was a proven fact. (The same is true of theories about the ozone layer and acid rain.) To describe it as a hypothesis is not necessarily to cast doubt on it, but to point to its status as one possible explanation of the limited evidence at our disposal. This is consistent, of course, with its being the best explanation to date. Nevertheless, not all experts agree about global warming, and it is worth rehearsing the areas of disagreement. There are, in fact, three: (1) the world is warming; (2) the cause of this is emissions created by humans; and (3) the effects of this will be major climatic change and substantial rises in sea level, leading to serious consequences for food production, housing, communications and so on.

Establishing the first of these claims is not nearly as easy as it sounds. We cannot simply place a thermometer in some suitable place. The measurements and calculations required are complex and hence open to varying interpretations and legitimate dispute. The second claim is even harder to prove satisfactorily. The global ecosystem is very large, not just in a geographical sense, but in terms of the number of factors operating on it. To isolate one of these factors is problematic. Nor is it a matter in which experimentation can be of much assistance. If industrial emissions are responsible for global warming, the process has been going on a long time. It cannot be reversed or turned off to see what difference this makes. It follows, that a great deal of conjecture is required. Let us suppose, nonetheless, that we are able to accommodate these difficulties and that the first two claims are as well established as we can hope to make them. The third claim is, if anything, fraught with still greater difficulties. This is partly because, unlike the other two, it involves prediction, and what is more, prediction on a very wide scale. The difficulty meteorologists have in predicting tomorrow's weather accurately is a salutary reminder of the degree of uncertainty that can be expected, and it should incline us to caution.

A major obstacle to accurate prediction about the effects of global warming is the known existence of what are sometimes called 'secular' climatic changes, that is, influences operating upon the system from without. We know that there have been ice-ages in the past. This is a fact of considerable importance here. It is not so long since climatologists were predicting the advent of another ice-age. Suppose that they were right, and that the hypothesis of global warming is also correct. One possible scenario is that the two cancel out, leaving the climatic future roughly similar to the present. This is one possibility. Another is that the impact of rising temperatures on the formation of ice and snow at the poles is to increase, not decrease it. The subject is complex, but some experts believe that this is a more likely outcome. A third area of discussion and disagreement revolves around the consequences for agriculture. Global warming may cause flooding and substantial loss of land. But it will also make temperate, areas of the earth that are currently intemperate, and hence make barren land productive. There will then be agricultural gains as well as losses. Whether the most likely result is net loss or net gain is a very complex question upon which, once more, the best informed are inclined to differ.

To recognize these difficulties in the way of making the three claims about global warming more than a hypothesis, is to acknowledge that the prediction of a crisis, of such proportions that the nations of the world have every reason to sink their differences, is much more speculative than is often imagined. If this is true, the sense of urgency on which the overriding claims of environmental ethics and politics depend is seriously weakened. To say this is not to detract from the science of ecology. Ecology has opened up new ways of thinking and set before us possible dangers of which, hitherto, we were unaware. Whether these possible dangers are *actual* is not a question that ecology properly so called can be expected to demonstrate. And what our response should be as human beings, citizens, or nations is a moral/political question, not a scientific one. Given the hypothetical nature of the claims we have been considering, care and caution would seem to be a more rational response than the invocation of crisis.

Many committed environmentalists regard reasoning of this sort as irresponsible. It seems to divert attention from what are to them very real and great dangers. The point to emphasize, however, is that they are right to regard it in this light only if there truly *is* a crisis, and this is just what is under dispute. An alternative reaction holds that, given the scale of the (admittedly) potential crisis, there can be no good reason to hesitate over taking precautionary steps. Is it not more rational to assume that we do face a crisis, and prepare for it, than to assume that there is not and remain unprepared?

Whether or not this is rational depends upon the cost and effectiveness of the precautionary steps proposed. Strategies intended to avert an anticipated environmental crisis are not cost free; electing to take these steps must be at the cost of something else. Second, their effectiveness to this end is never certain, and there is a danger of counterproductivity. Third, and perhaps most important, these costs may not fall evenly according to ability to bear them, so that it is not just rational self-interest which must be taken into consideration, but responsibility towards the poor.

Examples which illustrate all three points are not hard to supply. As an example of the first, consider energy saving policies designed to reduce carbon dioxide levels. Many of these have been supported by state subsidy, but the use of taxpayers' money to subsidize this, as opposed to increased medical facilities, say, is a political decision like any other about the best ways to use limited resources. The second point – possible counterproductivity – is a real prospect in certain recycling programmes. The recycling of glass, paper and metal is now a common feature of most Western societies, supported by the belief that recycling in some way reduces environmental costs and damage. But in at least some places, recycling glass is more expensive in terms of energy consumption than is making virgin glass, and in others, paper recycling has caused a reduction in the planting of just the sorts of trees which are most effective at removing carbon dioxide from the atmosphere.

The third point – about responsibility to the poor – is illustrated by one approach to the thinning of the ozone layer. When scientists first expressed anxiety about this, it was quickly suggested that part of the cause lay in substances known as CFCs, which were commonly used in aerosols for hair spray, deodorant, insect repellent and so on. An international moratorium on the manufacture and use of such chemicals was speedily agreed to. The danger that comes with the thinning of the ozone layer, it is thought, is an increased chance of skin cancer amongst fair skinned people, and the loss of one sort of deodorant spray seems a small price to pay. But the cost of ceasing to use CFCs was not confined to deodorants. It also meant abandoning a cheap form of refrigeration. Now, while this was of relatively little concern to users in developed countries, it did mean that the prospect of benefiting from refrigeration was lost to people in very poor countries, at least in the short to medium term. Moreover, since people in these countries were largely dark-skinned, the benefit of abandoning CFCs if these are construed exclusively or chiefly in terms of risk of skin cancer, do not accrue to these people. In this way, to urge the banning of CFCs was, arguably, to buy benefits for the relatively rich at the expense of the very poor.

These examples do not show, and are not intended to show, that energy saving is unimportant, recycling is a waste of time or that CFCs ought not to have been banned. All they show is that environmentally protective strategies such as these cannot simply be regarded as obvious, sensible precautions in the face of possible longer-term dangers. They are policies like any other, uncertain of success and with both financial and opportunity costs. In the absence of compelling evidence of the imminence of crisis, then, they must be considered on their merits, alongside any other policy.

So at least it can plausibly be argued, and, consequently, those who think that many ethical issues have to be re-thought along environmental lines are on weak ground if the only defence of their case is its urgency. The allegedly critical character of environmental concerns has not been demonstrated, and without such a demonstration we can only conclude that they are important, not that they are more important than any other.

One reply which environmentalists might make at this point is that this argument against environmental ethics begs the question because it has so far been conducted in terms of familiar, age-old political values such as social costs and benefits. To appreciate the truly radical character of a revisionary 'green' ethic, we should understand that the difference is not to be found in the introduction of a new set of problems, important though these are. It is not a new range of dangers that is radically different, but a new range of values – environmental values – in terms of which these dangers now need to be understood and assessed.

Deep Ecology

In the examples of the ozone layer, recycling and so on, the costs of adopting policies of the sort recommended by environmentalists were assessed in terms of human health and welfare. A depletion of the ozone layer is of concern because of increased risks of skin cancer. Recycling, when it works efficiently, saves natural resources for other economic purposes. To assess the costs and advantages of environmentally sensitive measures in this way puts them on a par with other political choices because it uses the common measure of human well-being. In this way it is anthropocentric, that is, it makes human interests the touchstone of value. For this reason it has sometimes been derided as a 'shallow' ecology, and contrasted with a quite different sort of assessment.

The terms 'shallow' and 'deep' ecology were coined in a famous essay by the Norwegian philosopher Arne Naess, 'The Shallow and the Deep', and have come to be used widely. They are somewhat misleading, however, because 'ecology' here does not mean the branch of science discussed in a previous section. It would be more accurate to say that the word 'ecology' in the expressions 'shallow ecology' and 'deep ecology', simply means an evaluative attitude to the biosystem that is the earth, and because talk of ecology *is* rather misleading here, the terms deep and light green are sometimes preferred. But in whichever terms we draw it, the point of the distinction is to mark a difference between the attitude that gives the biosphere an *instrumental* value, and one which gives it *intrinsic* value.

Shallow ecology attributes value and importance to the processes of nature only in so far as these are important for human welfare and interests. Such a view believes that global warming, if it is a reality, represents a danger because it threatens agricultural production and human habitations, that the depletion of the ozone layer is important because of the risk to human health, and that the value of recycling lies in the consequent economic saving that can be made. Now, if this is the proper, and the only way to think about these matters, then, though the investigations of ecologists, climatologists and so on are important and interesting, it is indeed true that nothing *profoundly* new has been introduced into deliberation on national or international affairs. All that has happened is that we have encountered new instances of old problems – the promotion and protection of human health and prosperity. This is why such an approach is called 'shallow'.

By contrast, a 'deep' approach is concerned with changes to the biosphere *in themselves* and not just to the extent that they work to the benefit or detriment of human beings. To think in this way is to hold that there are things of value and importance whose value does *not* lie in their connection with human interests, that there are strictly environmental values. From this point of view, shallow ecology is objectionable because it makes human beings the sole focus of value and thus expresses a kind of arrogant self-centredness.

But if there are environmental values, what are they, and what makes them values? One obvious candidate, though not one exclusively associated with the rise of environmental philosophy, is other animals. Are other animals to be valued solely in so far as they contribute to or detract from human welfare, or do they have a value in themselves? In the course of the nineteenth century, attitudes on this question underwent an important change, and the belief that other animals cannot be treated in any way which may serve or please human beings became widespread. It was under the influence of this altered belief that steps were taken to protect animals in law from unnecessary suffering, and organizations concerned with animal welfare sprang up.

It is not difficult to construct a plausible argument to this conclusion. It is widely accepted that causing pain to other people is wrong, and that any action which does so needs special justification. But why include the phrase 'to other people'? Surely the wrongfulness of such behaviour arises from the nature of pain. However, if this is agreed, it must also be agreed that other animals besides human beings can feel pain, from which it follows that causing pain to animals without justification must also be wrong. To insist on including the phrase 'to other people' is to be guilty of what has come to be known as 'speciesism', the ungrounded belief that causing pain to one's own species is wrong, while causing pain to members of another species is not. To say it is ungrounded, is to say that it is nothing more than a prejudice, and it is ungrounded because it invokes an irrelevant consideration. The only relevant consideration is ability to feel pain, and this is present in more than one species.

To press moral right and wrong beyond human boundaries, then, is not difficult, but the cause of animal welfare both predates anything properly called environmental philosophy and falls far short of the range of issues with which deep ecology is concerned. The question to be asked next, therefore, is whether this extension can be pressed still further and if so on what basis.

A suitably telling test case is wilderness, about which environmental philosophers have written extensively. There are still large areas of the earth's landmass which are uninhabited by human beings, and in the most inhospitable regions, by animals as well. Many of them are areas of great beauty and grandeur. Now, such things as global warming and acid rain could have major effects on these. If the ice caps were to melt significantly, for instance, this would mean not merely that cities in which human beings live would be submerged under water, or that polar bears and other animals would die for lack of a suitable habitat, but that the landscape itself would be drastically altered. A great change would have taken place, but would this change amount to a loss? If it would, then there is reason to think that steps ought to be taken to prevent it. If it would not, there is no reason to take such steps, and certainly not at the expense of anything else. To decide this issue, we need to ask what, if anything, would make it a loss?

It is difficult, but very important for the purposes of this argument, to find an explanation of the loss which is in no way anthropocentric. Areas of wilderness have, for a very few, recreational value. They are places to explore that provide exceptional experiences, and they may constitute places in which the human spirit is tested to extremes and shown at its most inspiring. Such is the case when, for example, Antarctica is crossed on foot unaided. It is arguable, though not altogether plausible given the vast expanse of the oceans, that the destruction of wilderness would bring such opportunities to an end. Wilderness may also have scientific value, that is, importance for the furthering of human scientific understanding. Or it may be the unknown repository of important resources – minerals, ores or oil. Claims of this kind are often made in its favour. But all of these explanations effectively cash out the value of wilderness in terms of human interests.

One explanation of the value of wilderness, which if it does this, does it much less obviously, appeals to its beauty. Can we not say that the destruction of the Arctic wastes would be the destruction of great beauty, and that beauty has intrinsic interest? A question might be raised about the allegedly intrinsic character of beauty. Does the value of beauty not depend ultimately on its being perceived and appreciated by human beings? One way of approaching this question is to ask whether it makes any sense to say that the elimination of the *beauty* of wilderness would be a loss to any other animals that might live there, polar bears for instance. That beauty is essentially subjective is a familiar theme in philosophy, and raises a number of complex issues. Without addressing these adequately, the most we could say is that the beauty of wilderness is a *possible* value which would make its alteration or elimination a loss. However, even without engaging in these issues, there is another factor that counts against this argument. Beauty is a value, let us agree, but it is not a peculiarly environmental value. There is beauty in much that is entirely made by humans, and the claims of beauty and its preservation predate contemporary concerns. That the elimination of the beautiful or the construction of the ugly are relevant to matters of public policy, both national and international, is hardly new or contentious, but equally, conceived in this way, beauty takes its place among a set of sometimes competing values between which choices must be made. If, for example, the wholesale industrialization of the underdeveloped world were to put in jeopardy the continuing existence of large areas of wilderness, the beauty that would be lost would have to be set alongside the elimination of poverty that would be gained. The choice might be hard, but it would not be new either in its scale or in the values that it brought into consideration.

The Gaia Hypothesis

It seems then that we are still in search of a truly environmental value. Deep ecologists, at this point, have turned to the integrity of the biosphere as a whole, and it is here that appeal is sometimes made to 'the Gaia hypothesis'. The Gaia hypothesis, which is associated with the work of the naturalist James Lovelock, is

not, as its name might suggest, a return to some variety of nature mysticism, but a serious scientific theory. We are inclined
to think of the earth as a physical system, with, as it were,
a biological covering of vegetable and animal organisms.
Lovelock's hypothesis is that certain puzzling phenomena in the
history of the natural world and in its functioning are better
explained if we regard the earth as a whole as itself an organism.
The relevant differentiating feature is adaptive recovery. If a
physical system is damaged, it is permanently changed, but an
organism has recuperative powers. It can respond to traumas in
ways which restore it to its former, normal, condition. So, at a
simple level, while broken rocks remain broken, torn flesh repairs
itself. What the hypothesis holds is that we will better explain
certain global processes if we think of them in terms of adaptive
response, than if we think of them as the mechanical workings of
a physical system.

This is not the place to speculate on the cogency of this
hypothesis. What is relevant here is the implication the Gaia
hypothesis has, if any, for the claim that there are distinctively
environmental values. Suppose that the hypothesis is true. This
would warrant us in saying that the biosphere as a whole is
an integrated organism, an organic entity. Does it follow that
there is special reason to respect it, or that there is reason to
abandon a range of human activities on account of their effects
upon it?

The answer to both questions seems to be no. With regard to
the first it seems trivial, but it is, in fact, relevant to remark, that
every tree is an organism with powers of adaptive recovery, but
that this does not imply that lumberjacks are murderers or even
vandals. Of course, it could be asserted that if the earth is an
organism, it is the largest organism there is, and the one on
which we depend for the only home we have. These two
remarks pull in different directions however. The appeal to Gaia
as home, draws us back once more to a consideration of (long
term) human interests. The remark about its size, if it is not
interpreted as a groundless worship of the large in and for itself,
gives ground for confidence rather than caution, and brings us to
the second question: the effects that we can have on it.

Lovelock himself entertains fewer fears for Gaia than many who have appealed to his hypothesis. This is because he thinks that the recuperative powers of Gaia are consonant with its size. He points out that we know from geological evidence that the earth faced huge challenges in the past – the massive changes in temperature which caused the ice-ages, and the cosmic storms which, some think, explain the disappearance of dinosaurs and other prehistoric creatures. But it survived them, and this provides reason to think that it can survive changes which, from our perspective, might appear to be catastrophic. This does not necessarily mean that all is well from a human point of view, for, as Lovelock also observes, if the survival of Gaia requires the elimination of human beings because of the effects of their activities, the chances are higher that the human race will be eliminated than that Gaia will be destroyed. From this it follows, of course, that we need not worry unduly about environmental damage *if* the basis of our concern is the well-being of Gaia.

International Politics and the Environment

It will be evident that the issues which this chapter has ranged over cannot be conclusively settled in such a small compass, involving as they do complex questions in science as well as philosophy. Some important lines of thought have been ignored. There is more to be said about interconnectedness, for example, especially in the light of the 'new' ecology parenthetically noted earlier, and biodiversity as a possible environmental value has not been discussed. Still, the argument seems to justify this provisional conclusion: the case for a distinctive environmental ethic has not been made. The combined effects of human actions and policies on an international scale are undeniably matters of importance, but their importance does not lie either in their extreme urgency, or in the special 'environmental' values they bring into play.

This is not such a negative conclusion as it might appear. It shows only that we have no reason to be *deep* green, and leaves the case for being *light* green unimpaired. In any case, what are commonly called environmental issues vary so enormously in character, that it would be surprising if we *could* find a single value or set of values underlying them all. It is not fanciful to suppose that there is a connection between global warming and the Gaia hypothesis, but it is fanciful to think that the Gaia hypothesis is importantly linked to conservation in historical town centres. Similarly, the growth of world population, if it is a problem, is a problem of quite a different order to the problem of litter on river banks.

In the light of such observations, it is more plausible to think that 'environmental issues' are not problems arising from a single source, but a variety of concerns brought under a single name, with this unifying element: 'environmental' issues refer not to the *internal* character of human lives – their health, nutrition, enjoyment and so on – but with the *external* environment in which those lives must be lived. This external environment can be of any scale – from the upper atmosphere and the surface of the earth with its wildernesses to the fish in local streams and the built environment immediately around us. Furthermore, though concern with the quality of this environment is necessarily connected with human interests, the connection need not be in the narrow sense of mere *usefulness* to human beings. I can want to live in conditions where birds and plants and animals are healthy, varied and plentiful, and the only way I can secure this desire is by giving prominence to the well-being of the other creatures in my environment.

This is worth stressing. It is a mistake to reject 'shallow' ecology on the grounds that it reduces the environment and all it contains to the status of disposable instruments to human ends. The natural world can be valued in other ways. The beauty of natural landscapes, and the scientific significance of parasites *literally* enrich my life and experience, though in wholly non-utilitarian (and non-economic) ways. Nonetheless, their value as sources of enrichment is an assessment made from a *human* point of view. Shallow ecology is humanist, and so falls short of the aspirations of the deep ecologist, but it is not vulgarly utilitarian, giving everything a cash value as it were, which is the ground upon which it is often declared shallow.

The discussion of this chapter so far has addressed the idea of environmental *ethics*. What is the connection between ethics and politics here? If the argument to this point has been sound, we must favour so-called shallow ecology over deep alternatives, and shallow ecology is humanist. Its humanism has this implication. Environmental concerns are not nugatory, but they are not mandatory either. They must take their place alongside all the other concerns which form the materials of political debate. Previous chapters have explored the moral or ethical limits and constraints on politics in the international arena. Where environmental issues bring important values into play, the same can be said of them – that they place moral or ethical constraints on politics. But they do not place overriding constraints. This is how it ought to be, in my view. We have encountered no reason for thinking that it should be otherwise and must take into account the fact that the interests which *conflict* with concerns about the environment can be very pressing.

Consider this example. The future of the African elephant is in serious jeopardy. Hunted for their ivory tusks on a huge scale, their numbers in many places are so seriously depleted that total extinction by the early decades of the next century is a real possibility (though in the interests of accuracy it should be recorded that the position varies considerably in different parts of Africa). Those who contemplate the uniqueness, magnificence and zoological interest of the largest land-based mammal on earth cannot but regard this prospect with alarm. Those who hunt and process the ivory, however, are for the most part poor, and cannot afford the luxury of contemplating the magnificence of the beasts from whom they wrest a not very lavish livelihood. It is hardly surprising, then, that the anticipated demise of the elephant rouses more passion in Europe and America than it does among the ordinary people of Kenya and Tanzania. If East African hunters had the articulacy of European campaigners, which in general they do not, they might respond to objectors in the following fashion.

We have to live, and we have to do so in a country with relatively few resources and virtually no industrial, commercial and financial base. Set against our need to live is the interest of Westerners in preserving wild life in game reserves, for photography, selective hunting and scientific study. Perhaps also there is something intrinsically desirable about preserving certain types of animal. If we had the alternative resources we too might think that the hunting of elephants for ivory should be banned. But we have not. The proposed ban on the ivory trade is good for the elephants and hence conducive to environmental sentiments. It represents a small price for Westerners (the unavailability of a luxury good). But it means the end of livelihood for many poor hunters and small businessmen in East Africa and Arabia. Why should our vital interests be destroyed to protect Western sensibilities? If the price to Westerners were what it is to us, the environmental lobby would have much less support.

In imagining this response I have necessarily simplified the issue, and it should not be supposed that this is the last word on the matter or, consequently, that the hunting of elephants for ivory ought not to be stopped. What it is intended to show is that identifying it, correctly, as an environmental concern is not the last word either. Appeals to deep ecology or the biosphere can distort the issue, which involves a profound conflict of interest and opinion. The example is specially instructive in this respect. It is easy, and accurate, to construe it as a clash between crude economic interest on the one hand and the preservation of the glories of nature on the other. Yet it is also a conflict between the poor, whose real choices are limited, and the rich who can entertain options at relatively little cost. It is the poor in this example, who are motivated by self-interest in the narrow sense, and the rich who are alive to wider, 'global' concerns. For all that, to claim paramount importance for *environmental* issues in international affairs, would in this instance be a case of surreptitiously sequestering the authority of the 'global' on the side of the rich in the distribution of international power.

The truth is that pursuing ethical policies in international affairs inescapably involves balances and trade-offs between the cardinal, but sometimes competing, values of peace, freedom, justice and welfare. The environment has an important part to play in both the conception and the realization of the last of these, but the impression is sometimes created that 'ecology' has raised these elements out of the general consideration of welfare and given them new and overriding status. What the arguments of this chapter have shown is that upon examination this impression is an illusion. The moral significance of the environment is no more important, but probably not less so, than the morality of war, deterrence, intervention, terrorism, basic rights, in short, all the other topics that make up ethics in international relations.

Suggestions for further reading

Andrew Dobson, *Green Political Thought.*
L. Gruen and D. Jamieson (eds), *Reflecting on Nature.* A useful collection of readings, which includes the Rio declaration.
Holmes Rolston III, *Philosophy Gone Wild: Environmental Ethics.*
Peter Singer (ed.), *A Companion to Ethics*, relevant entry: Robert Elliot, 'Environmental Ethics'.

Bibliography

Aiken, W. and Lafollette, H. (eds) 1977: *World Hunger and Moral Motivation*. Engelwood Cliffs: Prentice-Hall.

Augustine 1930: *Selected Letters*, tr. J. H. Baxter. London: Loeb Classical Library.

Bainton, Roland, H. 1960: *Christian Attitudes toward War and Peace*. Nashville: Abingdon Press.

Bauer, P. T. 1980: *Equality, the Third World and Economic Delusion*. London: Weidenfeld & Nicolson.

Beitz, C. R. 1979: *Political Theory and International Relations*. Princeton: Princeton University Press.

Brownlie, Ian (ed.) 1995: *Basic Documents in International Law*. Oxford: Clarendon Press.

Bull, Hedley 1977: *The Anarchical Society*. London: Macmillan.

Bull, Hedley 1984: *Intervention and World Order*. Oxford: Clarendon Press.

Conrad, Joseph 1995: *Heart of Darkness*, ed. Robert Hampson. London: Penguin Books.

Dobson, Andrew 1990: *Green Political Thought*. London: Unwin Hyman.

Ehrlich, Paul 1968: *The Population Bomb*. New York, Ballantine.

Frey, R. G. and Morris, Christopher (eds) 1991: *Violence, Terrorism and Justice*. Cambridge: Cambridge University Press.

Graham, Gordon 1990: *The Idea of Christian Charity*. Notre Dame: Notre Dame University Press.

Gruen, L. and Jamieson, D. (eds) 1994: *Reflecting on Nature*. Oxford and New York: Oxford University Press.

Hardin, Garrett 1974: 'Lifeboat Ethics: The Case Against Helping the Poor'. *Psychology Today*, 8, 38–43.

Hegel, G. W. F. 1952: *Philosophy of Right*, tr. T. M. Knox. Oxford: Clarendon Press.

Hobbes, Thomas 1960: *Leviathan*, ed. Michael Oakeshott. Oxford: Basil Blackwell.

Honderich, Ted 1980: *Violence for Equality*. Harmondsworth: Penguin Books.

Hopkirk, Peter 1990: *The Great Game*. Oxford: Oxford University Press.

Kedourie, Elie 1961: *Nationalism*, 2nd edition. London: Hutchinson.

Lackey, Douglas 1984: *Moral Principles and Nuclear Weapons*. Totowa: Rowman and Littleheld.

Locke, John 1960: *Two Treatises of Government*, ed. Peter Laslett. Cambridge: Cambridge University Press.

Lovelock, James 1986: 'Gaia: the World as Living Organism'. *New Scientist*, 28 (December).

McNeilly, F. S. 1968: *The Anatomy of Leviathan*. London: Macmillan.

McPherson, James, M. 1988: *Battle Cry of Freedom*. Oxford and New York: Oxford University Press.

Morgenthau, Hans 1954: *Politics Among Nations: The Struggle for Power and Peace*, 2nd edition. New York: Knopf.

Naess, Arne 1973: 'The Shallow and the Deep, Long Range Ecology Movement: A Summary'. *Inquiry*, 16, 95–100.

Nardin, Terry 1983: *Law, Morality and the Relations of States*. Princeton: Princeton University Press.

Nardin, T. and Mapel, D. R. (eds) 1992: *Traditions of International Ethics*. Cambridge: Cambridge University Press.

Nozick, R. 1974: *Anarchy, State and Utopia*. Oxford: Basil Blackwell.

O'Neill, Onora 1986: *The Faces of Hunger*. London: Allen & Unwin.

Ramsay, Paul 1968: 'The Limits of Nuclear War'. In *The Just War: Force and Political Responsibility*. New York: Bantam Books.

Rolston, Holmes III 1986: *Philosophy Gone Wild: Environmental Ethics*. Buffalo: Prometheus.

Rousseau, Jean-Jacques 1994: *The Social Contract*, tr. C. Betts. Oxford: Oxford University Press.

Seaman, L. C. B. 1964: *From Vienna to Versailles*. London: Edward Arnold.

Shue, Henry 1980: *Basic Rights*. Princeton: Princeton University Press.

Shue, Henry (ed.) 1989: *Nuclear Deterrence and Moral Restraint*. Cambridge: Cambridge University Press.

Simon, Julian L. 1980: 'Resources, Population, Environment: An Oversupply of False Bad News'. *Science*, 208, 1431–7.

Singer, Peter 1972: 'Famine, Affluence and Morality': *Philosophy and Public Affairs*, 1, 229–43.

Singer, Peter (ed.) 1993: *A Companion to Ethics*. Oxford: Basil Blackwell.

Teichman, Jenny 1986: *Pacifism and the Just War*. Oxford: Basil Blackwell.

Vincent, R. J. 1974: *Non-intervention and International Order*. Princeton: Princeton University Press.

Walzer, Michael 1977: *Just and Unjust Wars*. New York: Basic Books.

Warner, Martin and Crisp, Roger (eds) 1990: *Terrorism, Protest and Power*. Aldershot: Edward Elgar.

Weir, Alison 1995: *Lancaster and York: The Wars of the Roses*. London: Jonathan Cape.

Index

tragedy of the commons   141, 144
transfer of resources   34, 40–2
Treaty of Versailles (1919)   2

uncertainty   78, 121–2; *see also*
  certainties
unintended consequences   69
United Nations   10–11, 15, 95, 102,
  106
universalizability   35–6

values, instrumental   166;
  intrinsic   166; quantification of
  139–40
Vietnam War   54
violence   62–5, 122, 123, 124,
  125–6

war   43, 45–6, 118, 127–8; Christian
  attitudes to   48–52; conventional
  90–1; declaration of   61–2, 64; as
  defensive   53, 54; as evil   51, 52–
  3; as holy   51; *see also* civil war;
  insurrection; Just War
Wars of the Roses (1455–85)   75,
  127
Warsaw Pact   2
wealth *see* affluence
welfare   96, 97, 145, 146–9, 150,
  155, 161, 175
wilderness   168–9
Wilson, Woodrow   3
World War I (1914–18)   52, 54, 93
World War II (1939–45)   65, 75, 76,
  120